The Rolling Stones
The Illustrated Biography

The Rolling Stones
The Illustrated Biography

Jane Benn

Photographs by

Daily Mail

Trans
Atlantic
Press

Published by Transatlantic Press
First published in 2009
This edition published 2011

Transatlantic Press
38 Copthorne Road Croxley Green Hertfordshire WD3 4AQ

© Transatlantic Press
Photographs ©Associated Newspapers Archive

A catalogue record for this book is available from the British Library.

ISBN 978-1-907176-26-5

Printed and bound in China

Contents

Introduction

As rock 'n' roll arrived in Britain, five young men were about to make an indelible mark on the world of popular music. After the meteoric rise of the Beatles and the Liverpool beat explosion that followed, the Rolling Stones pioneered a grittier, blues-based rock 'n' roll that was a complete contrast to the Mersey sound. The band soon earned the disapproval of the establishment because of their many brushes with the law and frequent wild behaviour, all of which perpetuated their image as the notorious 'bad boys' of rock – a reputation they were more than happy to exploit.

The band first achieved success in Britain, but it wasn't long before they cracked the American market too. Their 1971 album *Sticky Fingers* was the first in a consecutive run of eight No.1 hit albums in the United States and in 1989 the group was inducted into the Rock and Roll Hall of Fame. Their music has always been exciting and innovative, but also demonstrated a great flexibility of style; over the last 40 years they have sold more than 200 million albums worldwide and in 2004 they made it to No.4 in *Rolling Stone* magazine's 100 Greatest Artists of All Time. Rolling Stones tours are legendary for their spectacular visual effects, and even today the "greatest rock 'n' roll band in the world'" is still going strong and packing stadiums across the globe, albeit it with a slightly changed line-up. And so the unfinished journey from rebellion to respectability continues on. As manager Andrew Loog Oldham once famously wrote, "The Rolling Stones are more than just a group –they are a way of life."

Part One

Not Fade Away

In the beginning

Left: Michael Philip Jagger was born into a middle-class family at the Livingstone Hospital, Dartford, Kent, in 1943. His interest in music really started to develop while he was attending Dartford Grammar School where his academic achievements culminated in 3 A-level passes, thus securing his place at the London School of Economics. Although he had no formal music training and did not know how to read music, he had begun playing rock and roll with friends from school in Dartford Church Hall.

It was a chance meeting on a train from Dartford to London in October 1961 which set in motion the story of The Rolling Stones. Mick Jagger and Keith Richards had already crossed paths when they attended Wentworth Primary School in the early 1950s, but it was the unplanned encounter between the pair that led to the formation of the iconic and enduring band. Keith soon joined Mick and his friend, Dick Taylor, in a group called Little Boy Blue and the Blue Boys.

Opposite: Keith had been on his way to art college when he bumped into Mick. Keith had no particular aspirations to be an artist, but believed that he would be able to develop his guitar playing in the creative college environment.

The band forms

Left: The original line-up of The Rolling Stones consisted of lead-vocalist Mick Jagger, guitarists Keith Richards, Brian Jones and Bill Wyman, drummer Charlie Watts and pianist Ian Stewart and the band's name was inspired by the 1950s Muddy Waters song, "Rollin' Stone".

The newly formed group played their inaugural gig using this name at London's Marquee Club on 12 July 1962. The Rollin' Stones soon morphed into The Rolling Stones As the band became established they were signed up by the flamboyant impresario Andrew Loog Oldham after he saw them perform at The Crawdaddy Club in Richmond, Surrey, in April 1963. The 19-year-old manager soon dispensed with pianist Ian Stewart, informing the band that six members would be too many for a pop group. Stewart remained with the band as road manager and occasional keyboard player until his death in December 1985.

Brian Jones joined the band after he was spotted by legendary jazz musician Alexis Korner. Setting the pattern for his unconventional life, he had fathered two children with different women by the time he was 17. However, his love of music was evident at an early age –his mother taught him to play the piano when he was very young and he had the ability to pick up and play many instruments

The quiet men

Opposite: The quiet, poker-faced drummer Charlie Watts was born and raised in Islington, North London. He often played drums for Blues Incorporated, a band led by Alexis Korner, who had set up a weekly R and B club in the Ealing Club, West London, in March 1962 – a venue which soon became famous for its pioneering and innovative influences. Charlie soon quit Blues Incorporated when he was persuaded to join The Stones in January 1963.

Right: Bill Wyman, born William George Perks in Lewisham, London, in 1936, was the oldest member of the band. He attended Beckenham and Penge Grammar School for Boys, where he took piano lessons, joined the choir and played the clarinet. He learned to play the guitar during his National Service and this spell in the army also gave rise to his adopted surname, Wyman, the name of one of the friends who served with him at the time.

June 1963: first single released

Above: This very early picture of the band belies the image the band were soon to cultivate with such vigour. Their first appearance on ABC-TVs *Thank Your Lucky Stars* was the only time the group appeared wearing identical outfits. Soon they would be famous for their eclectic, rather bedraggled style, which they combined with wild and energetic stage performances – leading to manager Andrew Oldham's famous comment, "Would you let your daughter go out with one?"

Opposite: Mick and Keith go shopping in Carnaby Street, London. Shortly after signing the group Andrew Oldham managed to negotiate a recording contract with Decca – the British record company which famously turned down the chance to sign The Beatles. In June 1963 The Stones' first single "Come On" was released. This Chuck Berry cover, backed with Muddy Waters' "I Want To Be Loved", made it into the UK charts at number. 21.

International success

Opposite: The band, seen here at the Montreux Television Festival in spring 1964, were now high-profile celebrities and as such were invited to many media events. They had embarked on their first UK concert tour in September 1963. Soon after this they released their second single, the Lennon-McCartney composition, "I Wanna Be Your Man". This gritty rendition reached number 12 in the UK charts and truly brought them to the attention of the record-buying public.

Right: Keith uses the back stairs at London Airport to evade over-enthusiastic fans as The Stones set off for their first US tour in June 1964. After the success of the single "Not Fade Away" and the release of their debut album, *The Rolling Stones*, at the end of 1963 the band was riding high. Their two concerts at Carnegie Hall in New York were a huge hit and they were as well received in the States as they had been in Britain.

Song-writing partnership

Opposite: An early picture of the Stones performing. The band's first number 1 single was followed swiftly by an equally successful EP *Five by Five* released in August and another chart-topping blues song, "Little Red Rooster", in November 1964. By this time the Jagger-Richards writing partnership was becoming more prolific, providing material for their own use and for other artists. Gene Pitney's recording of "That Girl Belongs to Yesterday" was the first song composed by The Rolling Stones songwriting duo to become a top-10 hit in the UK.

Right: Mick was soon appearing in the gossip columns and dating Chrissie Shrimpton, sister of the model Jean Shrimpton. However, 1964 was also a productive year for the band as they had completed four UK and two US tours. They also celebrated their first UK number 1 single, "It's All Over Now", in July of that year.

Fans riot

Above: The Stones were no strangers to controversy and had been dogged with a history of problems at live concerts. They had first experienced difficulties at Wembley Stadium in April 1964 when 30 fans were arrested for riotous behaviour and there were further issues in Scotland later in the year. This concert in Berlin in June 1965 was marred by rioting fans and 50 rows of seats were destroyed.

Opposite: Mick Jagger leaves a Liverpool court with co-manager Eric Easton after pleading guilty to three motoring offences. His licence was endorsed and he was fined £32 but he escaped disqualification from driving. Easton came to work with Andrew Oldham after Beatles manager Brian Epstein had turned down Oldham's suggestion that they manage the group together.

Charlie weds

Opposite: Charles Robert Watts married Shirley Ann Shepherd at a secret ceremony in Yorkshire on 14 October 1964. Soon after the wedding Charlie had to leave Shirley behind as he embarked on the second US tour of the year. The couple first met at an Alexis Korner gig, before Charlie became famous, and they remain together today. They have one daughter, Seraphina Watts, born on 18 March 1968.

Above: The band were voted the best British band in a *Melody Maker* poll and received their award at a Variety Club of Great Britain luncheon at London's Savoy Hotel in September 1964. Adding to their accolades, "Not Fade Away" was also named as best single of the year.

Birthday celebration

Above and opposite: Mick celebrates his 21st birthday on 26 July 1964 with fan Carolyn English at a hotel in Preston. As the pair toasted the occasion with a glass of orange juice, the Stones cover of American singer-songwriter Bobby Womack's "It's All Over Now" was climbing the UK charts. It soon reached the number-1 slot, where it remained for five weeks.

Crowd control continued to be a problem for the band; a few days before Mick's birthday festivities the Stones appeared at the Tower Ballroom in Blackpool and had to be rescued after rioting broke out during the show. They had to leave the stage, and all their equipment was smashed. In an effort to pre-empt similar trouble in Liverpool later in the year, the band hired 24 rugby players to protect them at the concert. However, thousands of fans still managed to overcome the guards and storm the stage.

An appearance with Ed Sullivan

Above: Brian and Keith depart for New York for their second American tour in October 1964. The tour coincided with the release of their second US album *12 x 5* on 17 October. While in the States the band made their first nationwide TV appearance on *The Ed Sullivan Show*, when an estimated 70 million viewers watched their performance. Their raunchy style did not go down well with the older generation, prompting Ed Sullivan to promise that they would never appear on his show again. However, they returned six months later!

Opposite: Mass hysteria gives rise to further problems as the band launch their third British tour in August 1964. Some policemen come to the rescue of their colleague Jacqueline Rooney who was injured on the stage as The Stones performed.

Mounting tensions

Above: The band relax between gigs in Scotland in June 1965. but rumours about their differences were spreading. During their third North American tour in May 1965 they recorded one of the most famous Jagger-Richards songs, "(I Can't Get No) Satisfaction". It soon went to number 1 in the States, where it spent four weeks at the top of the charts and established The Stones as a worldwide premier act. However, the tour was beset with problems causing tensions between Brian and Mick to escalate.

Opposite: Keith and Charlie enjoy a cup of tea outside a London magistrates' court in July 1965. The three other band members had been summonsed to face charges of insulting behaviour and using obscene language. Mick, Brian and Bill underlined their rebel credentials when they faced accusations of urinating against a wall in a petrol station after they had been refused permission to use the facilities.

Three number-1 hits

Opposite: Mick and Keith cheerfully leave the court after they had been fined £5. Despite their bad boy image 1965 was a very successful year for the band. Their chart-topping singles of the previous year were supplemented by three more number 1s in the UK – "The Last Time", "(I Can't Get No) Satisfaction" and "Get Off My Cloud" were all huge hits. The year also saw their first number 1 album success in the US with *Out of Our Heads*.

Right: The Stones pictured at yet another airport. They had rolled from one tour to another with little respite in 1965. There were also major changes in the personal relationships of some members of the group. Brian became inseparable from model Anita Pallenberg after meeting her backstage at a gig in Munich in September. Meanwhile, Mick's two-year love affair with Chrissie Shrimpton was on the wane, despite rumours that the couple were considering marriage.

Aftermath

Above: Four of the Stones pictured in New York during their fifth American tour in July 1966. The tour was supported by their album, *Aftermath*. The acclaimed album was the first to feature only Jagger-Richards compositions as well as the first to be recorded entirely in the States. The album soon rocketed to number 1 in the UK charts; it included "Paint it Black", which was released as a single in May and became an instant number 1 on both sides of the Atlantic.

Opposite: Mick photographed at the beginning of 1967 just after the release of controversial single "Let's Spend the Night Together" backed by the ballad "Ruby Tuesday". Although it created shockwaves in Britain, the song was not banned from the airwaves. However, the lyrics proved to be too much for the more conservative American public and when the band made their third appearance on *The Ed Sullivan Show*, they were instructed to change the words to "Let's Spend some Time Together".

Mick and Marianne

Left: By the time his relationship with Chrissie Shrimpton ended in December 1966 Mick was involved with singer Marianne Faithfull, another of Andrew Oldham's protégés. Her career was launched with the Jagger-Richards composition, "As Tears Go By", in June 1964 which reached number 4 in the UK charts. Marianne had previously been married to artist John Dunbar, with whom she had a son, Nicholas, in 1965.

Opposite: Body language tells the story – 1967 could be perceived as the Stones "annus horribilis" as a series of drug-related charges dogged the band for much of the year. There were growing tensions within the group – particularly between Mick and Brian who appeared to be embroiled in a wrangle over leadership. Brian was also becoming increasingly debilitated after his split with Anita Pallenberg, who had immediately embarked on a relationship with Keith.

Still smiling

Opposite: Mick Jagger is still smiling in May 1967. Despite their troubles the band continued with their heavy touring schedule. However, their reputation meant that they were closely scritinized by customs officials wherever they travelled and the police abroad were less than sympathetic towards them.

Above: Keith and Mick stand outside Chichester court on 10 May 1967, where they had been remanded on bail. Keith had been charged with allowing his premises to be used for the consumption of illegal substances in February 1967 whilst Mick, together with friend and art dealer Robert Fraser, faced the lesser charge of possession.

Drugs raid

Left: Police had raided Redlands, Keith Richard's moated Sussex house, after the *News of the World* newspaper had erroneously reported that Mick Jagger had admitted taking LSD. In fact the reporter who penned the story had been talking to Brian Jones in a dimly lit night club and mistaken him for the lead singer of the band! The amphetamines that police found in the jacket said to belong to Mick were actually Marianne's but Mick insisted that he should take responsibility.

Opposite: Mick and Keith put a brave face on it as they leave Redlands for their court appearance. Brian Jones had also been due to visit Keith's home on the day of the arrest but was quickly telephoned and warned to stay away after the police arrived. However, his own London flat on Courtfield Road was raided on the same day as Jagger, Richards and Fraser appeared in court. Jones was also charged with possession of a number of illegal substances and allowing his home to be used for the consumption of drugs.

Mick and Keith face prison

Above: A quick break for the infamous pair as the court adjourned for lunch. Police had to clear a crowd of screaming fans out of the way before they could venture outside. Bill and Charlie were not involved in any of the court cases and were therefore able to spend some time working on their next album – eventually to be released at the end of 1967 as *Their Satanic Majesties Request*.

Opposite: On 29 June Keith Richards was given a one-year jail sentence and sent to Wormwood Scrubs prison together with Robert Fraser who received six months. Jagger was sentenced to three months imprisonment and dispatched to Brixton Prison. The next day the strain clearly shows when the pair were both bailed at £5,000 pending appeals against their convictions. Robert Fraser spent four months in jail after his appeal was denied.

Support from the Establishment

Left: Although many of the public felt that the men had "got what they deserved", there was a great deal of criticism in the press about the severity of the sentences imposed. *The Times* published a supportive editorial written by William Rees-Mogg entitled "Who Breaks a Butterfly on a Wheel". Most of the other newspapers followed suit and condemned the sentences – with the notable exception of the *News of the World*.

Opposite: Following the press attention the appeal was brought forward to 31 July. Keith was unable to attend as he was suffering from chickenpox and did not therefore hear the good news that his conviction had been quashed. Mick's relief is evident as his sentence was altered to a one-year conditional discharge.

Back in action

Above: The Jagger-Richards partnership was back in action but the pair had much to think about on their release. Immediately after his discharge Mick took part in a televised debate on the programme *World in Action*. The Bishop of Woolwich, politician Lord Stow-Hill and William Rees- Mogg were among the guests. Many people were surprised by Jagger's ability to articulate his argument with such clarity and intelligence.

Opposite: Putting the last few months behind him Mick looks happy as he leaves for New York in September 1967. The previous month had seen the release of "We Love You", a Jagger-Richards song featuring John Lennon and Paul McCartney on vocal harmonies. It was seemingly written to their fans as a message of thanks for the support given throughout the drug busts but also had undertones of defiance towards the police.

"As Tears Go By"

Left: Mick and Marianne. Andrew Oldham had noticed her at a party when she was just 17 years old and asked the Jagger-Richards pair to write a song for her, which resulted in the soulful ballad, "As Tears Go By".

Opposite: Brian heads off to New York in September 1967. His drug trial took place in November 1967. He was found not guilty of possessing cocaine and methedrine, but was convicted of cannabis possession and allowing his premises to be used for the consumption of illegal substances. He was initially given a nine-month prison sentence which was commuted to three years' probation on appeal and ordered to seek professional help.

Brian's last show

Left and opposite: On 12 May 1968 the group made a surprise appearance at the *NME* Poll Winners' Show at Wembley Arena and performed "Jumpin' Jack Flash" for the first time. The song was released two weeks later and flew straight to the top of the charts in the UK – the first number 1 single for the band for two years. This concert also marked Brian's last live show with the band as he continued to battle his demons.

"Jumpin' Jack Flash" has since reached iconic status; the band has played it during every tour since its release and it is the song most often played in concert. It has also been used in many films and television shows, including the 1986 Whoopi Goldberg comedy film of the same name. In fact the soundtrack includes two versions of the song; one by The Rolling Stones and a cover version by "Queen of Soul", Aretha Franklin.

Country pursuits

Above: A pensive Charlie enjoys spending time on country pursuits with wife Shirley as the couple share a passion for horses. Shirley had studied sculpture at art college and still continues to pursue her interest as an amateur sculptor. She had once famously said of her introspective husband, "Charlie's not really a Stone, is he? Mick, Keith, Brian, they're the big bad Rolling Stones".

Opposite: Brian had further run-ins with the law in May 1968 as he was again arrested on suspicion of possessing cannabis. He appeared in court on 26 September where he was found guilty of the charges and fined £50 plus costs. Although the sentence was surprisingly lenient for this second drug offense, it added to Brian's feelings of despair and depression.

Friendly rivals

Opposite: Brian is pictured with John Lennon, Yoko Ono and John's son Julian in December 1968. Despite speculation about the rivalry between the two bands, they were in reality good friends and often supported and influenced each other during the years of friendly competition. Brian had played alto saxophone on the Beatles song "You Know My Name (Look Up the Number)", and Mick and Keith contributed to the backing vocals on the famous anthem "All You Need is Love". Lennon and McCartney had of course provided The Stones with their first top twenty hit, "I Wanna Be Your Man". Above: Brian with tour manager Tom Keylock and girlfriend Suki Poitier.

Part Two

Street Fighting Men

In court again

Above and opposite: Mick Jagger and Marianne Faithfull had hoped for a more peaceful year following the turbulent events of 1968 and Marianne's miscarriage in November. However, there were further troubles ahead for the glamourous couple as drug charges were brought against them after a police raid on their Chelsea home in Cheyne Walk on 28 May 1969. They appeared at Marlborough Street Magistrates' Court the next day to face charges of possession of illegal substances and they were released on bail until 23 June. The police had claimed that they had found heroin, LSD and marijuana on the premises though Jagger maintained that any drugs found had been planted. When the case finally came to court he was fined £200 for possession of cannabis.

Brian is replaced by Mick Taylor

Opposite: On 8 June 1969 Mick, Keith and Charlie set off to visit Brian at his Cotchford Farm home in Sussex. Ostensibly the visit was to discuss the future of the band, but there was no surprise at the outcome of the visit as Brian and the band agreed to part company citing "musical differences". Two days later a 22-year-old veteran of John Mayall's Bluesbreakers, guitarist Mick Taylor, was recruited to replace Brian.

Above: Keith with girlfriend Anita Pallenberg. Keith and Anita had been together since March 1967 when some of the band travelled to Morocco on holiday in order to escape the furore over their drugs trial. During this trip the stormy relationship between Jones and Pallenberg escalated until Anita had had enough and embarked on an affair with Keith as Brian fell ill and was hospitalized.

Brian found dead

Left: A recently-divorced Bill with a friend at Brian's funeral. Within a month of Mick Taylor joining the band Brian Jones was dead. He had been found at the bottom of the swimming pool at his Cotchford Farm on the night of 2 July 1969. The official coroner's verdict on the incident was death by accidental drowning under the influence of drugs and alcohol, but there is still much debate and controversy surrounding his untimely death. The funeral took place Brian's home town of Cheltenham on 10 July and all the Stones attended, except Mick who was filming in Australia.

Opposite: The new line up of The Rolling Stones featured the handsome, rather self-effacing Mick Taylor. Mick was born in Hatfield, Hertfordshire, on 17 January 1947 and had been inspired to play the guitar by one of his uncles. His presence in the band was a significant factor in the riff-driven sound that is now so indelibly linked with the Stones.

Disaster at Altamont

Right: Keith and Charlie return from the American tour of 1969, which was to end in tragedy. The Stones' final concert at Altamont in California on 6 December 1969 was intended to be the US equivalent of the band's free Hyde Park concert in England earlier in the year when the Hell's Angels had provided the security. Unfortunately a young man named Meredith Hunter, became involved in an altercation with some members of the gang and was stabbed to death. By the end of the concert three more people were dead and hundreds injured.

Opposite: Jagger's introduction to acting in Nicholas Roeg's film *Performance* in 1968 had sparked his interest in films and in the summer of 1969 he and Marianne Faithfull travelled to Australia to film the movie *Ned Kelly*. Unfortunately the catalogue of troubles in his personal life continued when Marianne Faithfull took a massive overdose of sleeping pills and fell into in a coma for several days.

At home in Chelsea

Above: Keith and Anita relax at their Chelsea home in December 1969. The couple lived at 3 Cheyne Walk – a few doors down from Mick who lived at number 48. Their baby son Marlon had been born at King's College Hospital on 10 August 1969. Despite constant enquiries about their plans, the couple never married although they remained together for more than ten years.

Opposite: Mick Jagger outside the London court where he and Marianne Faithfull had been summoned to appear on 19 December. The couple pleaded not guilty to a charge of possessing cannabis. The court case had been delayed several times while Jagger and Faithfull were in Australia filming *Ned Kelly*. Jagger was fined £200 for possessing cannabis and made to pay 50 guineas costs. The charges against Faithfull were dismissed.

Let It Bleed

Opposite and above: The band, with new guitarist Mick Taylor, pose before their concert at the Saville Theatre in December 1969.The Stones had just released their new album *Let It Bleed*, a follow up to the 1968 album *Beggar's Banquet*. The new album was acclaimed by the critics and reached number 1 in the UK album charts, knocking the Beatles' *Abbey Road* off the top of the top slot. Two of the tracks featured Brian Jones on autoharp. The surreal cover of the LP featured a grotesque cake designed by Robert Brownjohn, a graphic designer known for his work with sixties pop culture. This was the last album the Stones released on the Decca label.

A difficult year

Above: The band performs on stage at the Lyceum Ballroom in London on 21 December 1969. This was part of a mini-tour of the UK to round off the year before Mick travelled to Rome to try to rekindle his relationship with girlfriend Marianne Faithfull. 1969 had been a difficult and challenging year for The Stones, both personally and professionally. The group had undergone a change in line-up and they had cut back on touring to spend more time in the studio. It was some consolation that their sole single of the year, "Honky Tonk Women", and only album released, *Let It Bleed*, both reached number 1 in their respective UK charts.

Opposite: Mick tries to shield Marianne Faithfull from the huge crowd of photographers who had come to report the results of the court case. By the time the case reached court their relationship was on the wane as Marianne had become involved with an Italian film director.

Farewell Marianne

Above: Marianne was increasingly dependent on drugs by the end of 1969 and her relationship with Mick was soon to come to an end. Her personal life quickly went into decline and her career went into a tailspin. She resorted to living on the street and soon lost custody of her son as a consequence. She eventually made a successful comeback in the late 1970s when she re-invented herself as a smokey-voiced survivor.

Opposite: Jagger and two other actors pose in Australian policemen's uniforms in a publicity shot for the movie *Ned Kelly* which starred Jagger in the title role. The film was directed by Tony Richardson and told the story of an Australian bushranger and folk-hero. There were many protests about the casting of Jagger as the legendary figure, both from Ned Kelly's descendants and from the actors' union Equity.

Enter Bianca

Opposite: Mick Jagger en route to Sweden during the band's 1970 European Tour. The series of concerts which started in Scandinavia on 30 August and finished in Amsterdam on 9 October, was the first in Europe since 1967. It was on this tour of Europe that Mick first met Bianca Perez Morena de Macia at a party after a concert. Bianca, who was born in Managua,

Nicaragua, in 1945, was studying political science in the city after winning a university scholarship.

Above: The Stones on stage at the Palais de Sports in Paris on 23 September – the second of their three gigs in the French capital.

Farewell to Britain

Opposite: Mick Jagger in familiar pose on stage in the band's "Farewell to Britain Tour" in March 1971. Following this first tour in their homeland since 1966, the group announced that they were moving to the South of France. Although many theories were expressed about this defection, the band always denied that their decision had anything to do with tax avoidance. After endless discussions and clashes, The Stones' contract with Decca had finally expired in July 1970; they signed a deal with Atlantic Records which allowed them to release songs on their own Rolling Stones label. *Sticky Fingers*, issued in April, was their first release on the new label.

Above: Mick and Bianca photographed in London. The couple had married in St Tropez on 13 May 1971 when Bianca was four months pregnant. The ceremony was attended by celebrities including Paul and Linda McCartney, Ringo Starr and Eric Clapton and numerous photographers. The Queen's cousin, photographer Lord Lichfield, gave away the bride. The public were somewhat hostile towards Bianca and did not warm to her lofty detachment.

Sporting pleasures

Above: Mick indulges his passion for cricket at a match on 11 August 1972. The previous month, Mick had celebrated his 29th birthday at a party with celebrity guests including Truman Capote, Bob Dylan, Andy Warhol and Carly Simon. A few days later he announced that he would retire from rock 'n' roll at the age of 33.

Opposite: Bill Wyman leaves for a skiing holiday with son Stephen and his new girlfriend Astrid Lundstrom. Wyman was far more circumspect than some other band members when it came to the use of alcohol and drugs, but was, by his own admission, "girl mad".

In fashion

Opposite: Mick and Bianca appear at a charity fashion gala at The Savoy Hotel in London in January 1973. The couple had just returned from a rescue mission to Bianca's native Nicaragua following a devastating earthquake on 23 December 1972. The Stones were soon to stage a benefit concert in Los Angeles to raise funds for the victims of the disaster. This concert served as a warm-up for their Pacific tour and raised more than £200,000 in relief funds.

Right: Mick and Bianca photographed in less formal attire.

Goats Head Soup

Left Mick assumes a detached air in his Vienna hotel room as the group embark on their two-month European tour in September 1973. The tour followed the release of their latest album *Goats Head Soup* on 31 August. This was a follow-up to their *Exile on Main Street* LP, released in May 1972 and now hailed as a masterpiece. Both these albums topped both the UK and US album charts.

Probably the best known track on *Goats Head Soup* was the guitar-driven ballad "Angie", written mainly by Keith Richard. The single, released in August 1973, became a phenomenal success and was the band's first US number 1 single since "Honky Tonk Women" five years previously.

Opposite: Mick strums his acoustic guitar, although he rarely played the instrument on stage.

Sell-out gigs

Left: Following performances in Vienna and West Germany in the autumn of 1973, the band returned for a series of concerts in the UK. Mick's aggressive posturing and the band's rebellious image continued to attract sell-out audiences for all the gigs.

Opposite: Keith pictured with his son Marlon. Keith and Anita also had a daughter, Angela (called Dandelion), born in Switzerland in May 1972. The couple were to suffer a personal tragedy in June 1976 when their third child Tara died of respiratory problems when he was only 10 weeks old.

Letting rip

Opposite: Mick lets rip in one of several tour dates in Wembley on the 1973 European tour. The band's anti-authoritarian attitude was symbolized by the now famous "lapping tongue and lips" logo which appeared on every record release. The design icon was created by Mick Jagger and graphic designer John Pasche – not Andy Warhol as is often believed – and soon became the most instantly recognizable symbol in rock.

Left: A pensive Mick Jagger – by the autumn of 1973 there were rumours that his marriage was faltering. He and Bianca had celebrated the birth of daughter Jade in Paris on 21 October 1971 while the band was in the process of recording *Exile On Main Street* in the south of France. Mick's first child, Karis, had been born to singer Marsha Hunt in November the previous year, although it was to be two years before he publicly acknowledged paternity.

Sell-out tour

Opposite: A leather-clad Mick Jagger works the crowd at the Empire Pool, Wembley on 7 September 1973. All their shows were complete sell-outs and hundreds of fans desperately tried to gatecrash by circulating among the 10,000 ticket holders.

Above: Mick demonstrates his agility in one of the Wembley shows. He had been voted one of the 100 best dressed men in the world in a magazine poll in March 1970. During later tours Mick cultivated an overtly sexual image with his slinky, tight outfits and laced lycra jumpsuits, often displaying a wide expanse of smooth chest.

More trouble for Keith

Opposite: Keith accompanies Mick as the phenomenon of the Stones rolls on at Wembley. The rhythm guitarist was awaiting the resolution of his most recent court case. He had been charged with possession of not only drugs but also firearms, when police had raided his London home on 26 June 1973. He was eventually fined £205 and given a conditional discharge when he attended Great Marlborough Street Magistrates' Court in October of the same year.

Right: The facial resemblance between Mick and Bianca was often remarked on. Despite her frivolous, party-going image Bianca was very much a political animal. She had campaigned against the corrupt Somoza regime in Nicaragua in the early 1970s and was afraid to return to her home country until the demise of the political dynasty in 1979.

It's only rock 'n' roll

Right: Mick pictured in May 1974 wearing one of the rhinestone-studded jumpsuits he favoured at this time. Soon after this, the band released the lead single from the near-namesake parent album, *Its Only Rock 'n' Roll (But I Like It)*. Released in July 1974, the record reached number 16 in the States and number 10 in the UK singles chart – the lowest chart placing since their first chart successes in 1963.

Opposite: The modest, rather introverted, bass guitarist Bill Wyman grew up in one of the less affluent areas of Sydenham in south-east London. He had started his musical career playing the organ with his father and learnt to play the piano at the age of 10. When he later taught himself to play the bass guitar he decided this was definitely the instrument for him.

Part Three

Maybe The Last Time

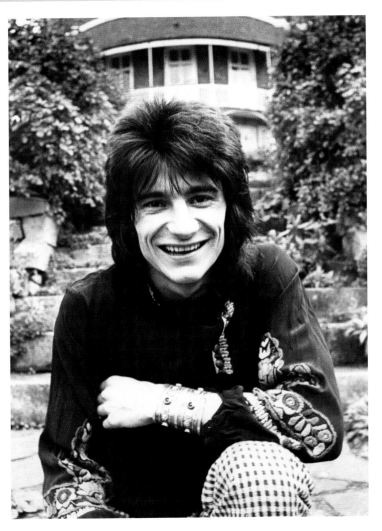

Ronnie replaces Mick Taylor

Left: Ronnie Wood initially joined the Stones on a temporary basis in April 1975. Mick Taylor had long been disenchanted with his position in the band and felt that his contributions were not valued sufficiently. This led to his departure at the end of 1974, soon after the release of his last album with the group, *It's Only Rock 'n' Roll*.

The affable Ronnie Wood had begun his musical career with The Birds in 1964. When the group disbanded in 1967, he joined the Jeff Beck Group along with singer Rod Stewart. After several tours with them the pair then joined the Small Faces, soon to reform as the Faces, where Ronnie was known for his distinctive guitar work as well as co-writing many of their songs.

He had been on friendly terms with the Stones for some years and was initially asked to help out on their Tour of the Americas in June 1975. He was the perfect foil for the unreliable Keith Richard, who had constantly clashed with Mick Taylor. The Faces announced their break-up in December 1975, and Wood was officially pronounced a member of the Rolling Stones soon after. Opposite: Ronnie Wood pictured with his wife Krissie.

Tour of the Americas

Opposite: Mick's fascination with the glamorous side of touring was reflected in his make-up and stage outfits as The Stones' biggest ever tour, Tour of the Americas, started at Louisiana State University, Baton Rouge, on 1 June 1975. The band played a series of 58 concerts to 1.5 million people across North America, finishing in Buffalo, New York, on 8 August.

Left: Mick uses his familiar pout on stage in April 1975. During the mid '70s many albums were produced by "The Glimmer Twins" – a pseudonym for Mick and Keith's rock-star partnership. The songwriting pair had adopted the name following an earlier South American trip when fellow passengers, unsure of their identity but believing they were glamorous celebreties, had asked them to "Give us a glimmer". *It's Only Rock 'n' Roll* was the first LP released using this nickname.

An exhausting schedule

Opposite: With so many concerts scheduled, the lead vocalist started to suffer with throat and larynx problems. Unusually, at a time when tours were considered a mechanism for promoting albums, the Tour of the Americas was not tied to the support of any newly released material. The band put out the compilation album, *Made in the Shade*, which only contained post-Decca compositions as the rights to their 1960s songs were owned by their former business manager Allen Klein.

Right: Mick performs on stage in Cleveland, Ohio. At the same time as *Made in the Shade* was released, Allen Klein put out a collection of songs under the title *Metamorphosis*. The album had been compiled without the band's involvement and consisted of a collection of outtakes and alternative recordings they had been obliged to hand over as part of the settlement when they sacked him.

More trouble with the law

Opposite: Keith looks relaxed before a concert in Baton Rouge, Louisiana. However, the American tour was not all plain sailing for the lead guitarist as he was arrested in Arkansas on 5 July while travelling from Memphis to Dallas with fellow Stones member Ronnie Wood. He was charged with reckless driving and carrying a concealed weapon. The knife charge was later dropped and Richard was fined $162.50 after pleading guilty to the driving charge.

Left: Mick in America. The tour was originally planned to cover South America as well as the northern continent, but a combination of currency fluctuations and concerns over security meant that concerts scheduled for Mexico, Brazil and Venezuela were cancelled.

Announcing their tour

Opposite: The grandiose American tour had been announced in typical ostentatious fashion when the band performed "Brown Sugar" while driving down New York's Fifth Avenue on the back of a flatbed truck. Their flamboyant tactics continued when the concerts started and included extravagant, outrageous props and a stage designed as a lotus plant which opened at the beginning of the shows to reveal the band inside.

Right: Following the Tour of the Americas, the band continued their punishing schedule with the Tour of Europe '76 which started in April. Keith is pictured at one of the Earls Court concerts in London where he often appeared in a zombie-like trance as he was so strung out on heroin. It was after one of the concerts at this venue that Keith learned that his 10-week-old baby son Tara had died. Despite being devastated by the tragedy, Keith insisted that the tour continue.

Ronnie's debut tour

Left: Mick supports Ronnie on stage as the most recent band member continues to learn the riffs and words for all The Stones songs. There had been a huge demand for tickets to see the 1976 tour of Europe and Great Britain. Applications for the three Earls Court shows in June exceeded one million and three extra shows were subsequently added.

Opposite: Mick and Keith share a microphone. The tour coincided with the release of the album *Black and Blue*. Although the funk and reggae influenced album only reached number 2 in the UK charts, it spent four weeks as number 1 in the US *Billboard* chart. However, reviews of the band's latest offering were very mixed; legendary rock critic Lester Bangs was to dismiss the LP as "the first meaningless Rolling Stones album".

Mesmerizing performances

Opposite: Mick gives an electrifying performance on stage at Earls Court. The Stones' shows always delivered an elaborate spectacle to their mesmerized audiences, helped by the use of an eclectic range of props varying from a suspended 80-foot silk dragon to clowns, confetti and even cannon fire.

Right: The lead single from the *Black and Blue* album, "Fool to Cry", featured in the set list for the European tour. Another Jagger-Richards composition, the ballad became a worldwide hit, although it only reached number 6 in the UK singles chart. It has been reported that Keith Richards was in such a bad state during the the tour that he fell asleep on stage while playing this song in Germany!

Showman

Left: The athletic Mick Jagger is the consummate showman on stage and consistently puts all his energy into his dynamic performances. At the series of Earls Court concerts he gradually stripped off items of clothing throughout the show until he was naked to the waist by the finale.

Opposite: Ronnie Wood relaxes at his Richmond home early in 1976. His wife Krissie, whom he married in 1971, was six months pregnant with son Jesse, born later that year on 30 October. Ronnie was born in Hillingdon, London, in 1947 and is a talented artist as well as a musician. His two brothers also demonstrated both artistic and musical talents; his older brother Art was lead singer in a sixties R & B group, The Artwoods.

Back in court

Opposite: Yet another drug-related court appearance for Keith Richard in January 1977. The white-faced Stone had been arrested in May 1976 after he crashed his Bentley on the M1 near Newport Pagnell and police found LSD and cocaine in the wreckage. Anita and son Marlon had been in the car when the accident happened, but were unhurt despite the fact that the car was written off.

Right: Mick flew in from Los Angeles to attend the court hearing at Aylesbury Crown Court in Buckinghamshire and offer support to his long-time friend. The apprehensive-looking lead guitarist had pleaded not guilty to all the charges. Mick sat in the public gallery throughout the three-day trial and watched intently as Keith took the witness stand.

Lonely Stone

Left: Mick attends the Bond Street Jubilee Ball in London's Berkeley Square to celebrate the Queen's Silver Jubilee on 7 July 1977. Bianca did not accompany him to the grand occasion, fuelling rumours about problems within their marriage.

Opposite: Smiles all around as a very relieved Keith celebrates with Mick in a local hotel. He had been found not guilty of possessing LSD, but guilty of possession of cocaine and fined £750 plus costs. However, he was soon to be in trouble again as he and Anita travelled to Toronto in February. Anita was arrested at the airport when a quantity of drugs was found in her luggage. A few days later, the Royal Canadian Mounted Police raided Keith's hotel room where they found the comatose Stone plus enough drugs to charge him with the extremely serious charge of drug trafficking – a crime that carried a maximum life sentence.

Love You Live

Opposite: The band's new album *Love You Live* was launched at London's Marquee Club in the summer of 1977. Mick again attended without Bianca but denied they were splitting up. The double live album was drawn from Tour of the Americas in 1975, the European Tour in 1976 and club shows from Toronto in 1977.

Above: The Stones minus Keith, who was unable to attend the launch party at The Marquee as he was undergoing drug rehabilitation therapy in the States after his arrest in Toronto. He lived under threat of criminal prosecution until the case finally came to court in October 1978 when he was given a year's suspended sentence and ordered to give a charity concert the following year.

Charlie flies solo

Opposite: The lugubrious Charlie Watts is at his most relaxed when doing what comes naturally. He has always been a huge fan of jazz and in 1964 he published an illustrated book about the legendary Charlie Parker entitled *Ode to a High Flying Bird*. In the late 1970s he joined Stones founding member Ian Stewart and Bob Hall in the boogie-woogie band, Rocket 88 which then released a live record of a concert in Germany.

For the Stones, the release of the album *Some Girls* in 1978 revalitzed their career. The LP incorporated the punk influences that were so significant at the time and became their biggest-selling album to date. It was the first album in 15 years on which Keith added the 's' back to his surname (making him "Richards") since Andrew Oldham had suggested he drop it in 1963.

Right: A cheerful Mick Jagger looks unperturbed by the preliminary divorce proceedings as he attends the High Court in London in May 1979. Bianca had started divorce proceedings as a result of Mick's involvement with Jerry Hall. Bianca's lawyer was the infamous "palimony" lawyer Marvin Mitchelson, who had represented Marsha Hunt in her paternity suit against Mick in 1972.

Mick's new love

Opposite: Mick with his new belle, the leggy Texan model Jerry Hall. The couple had first met when she was with Bryan Ferry, lead singer of Roxy Music. Jerry Hall's modelling career began in France in the early 1970s and her trademark long blond hair and commanding height soon ensured she was one of the most photographed models of the time.

Right: Mick sports a shorter hairstyle on stage at Shea Stadium, New York, during the 1981 American Tour. The three-month tour covered cities across the length and breadth of the States. In fact it was impossible to keep up with demand for tickets and many additional concerts were added to the original schedule.

September 1981: US tour kicks off in Philadelphia

Opposite and above: The tour kicked off at the JFK Stadium in Philadelphia on 25 September 1981. Mick used all his experience to whip up the enormous crowd on a very hot day. It was estimated that the amount of energy he expended on stage in a typical gig was equivalent to a 20-mile run!

The tour was used as a means of promoting the band's latest album, *Tattoo You*. This eclectic LP contained little in the way of new material and mainly consisted of an assembly of outtakes and ideas stretching back to *Goats Head Soup*. However, it proved to be a big commercial success and reached number 1 in the US album charts.

"Start Me Up"
Opposite and left: Mick belts
out another number in
Philadelphia as guitarist
Ronnie Wood concentrates on
his fretwork in the background.
The adventurous stage sets,
supported by vibrant props,
were particularly suited to the
outdoor concerts which mainly
took place in the daytime.

The band had released their
latest single "Start Me Up"
shortly before the beginning of
the American tour. It was
originally recorded with a
reggae beat and was the
opening song on the *Tattoo
You* album. With it's infectious
riff, the single sold over a
million copies in the first week
of its release and is still often
used as an opening song in
Stones' live shows.

Fifty-million-dollar tour
Left: Thirty-eight-year-old Mick is in full swing in front of the oldest band member Bill Wyman, who celebrated his 45th birthday with a party at Disneyworld in Florida while in the States. The American tour was estimated to have grossed $50 million in ticket sales with further income from merchandise. The group had also secured an innovative sponsorship deal with the Jovan perfume company who paid to have their name on the Rolling Stones tickets.

Tattoo You followed swiftly on the heels of *Emotional Rescue* which had been released in mid 1980. *Tattoo You* had been recorded among growing tensions and differences in personal ambitions within the band – particularly between Mick Jagger and Keith Richards. Although it was a commercial success it was another album which was panned by the critics. Opposite: Mick with Ronnie in the background.

Reaching bigger audiences

Opposite: Mick dons his bright puffer jacket before later stripping it off in the Philadelphia concert. The lucrative US tour also raised money through the sale of TV and movie rights. In another first, the band's performance at the Hampton Coliseum, Virginia, in December was broadcast on pay-per-view and in closed circuit cinemas and Hollywood director Hal Ashby, a Rolling Stones fan, accompanied the group on the tour, filming the documentary *Let's Spend the Night Together* which was eventually shown on cable TV.

Above: Bill's relationship with Swede Astrid Lundstrom was the most enduring of his love affairs – they were together for nearly 17 years and finally split in 1983. The 1980s saw Bill's solo career take off when he released the single "(Si,Si) Je Suis Un Rock Star" in July 1981 which went on to become a top 20 hit. He had already released three solo albums which were not commercially successful but had received many positive reviews.

Dressed to impress

Opposite: Mick and Keith rock on at Wembley Stadium in June 1982 in their first European tour for six years. When performing Mick usually favoured bright primary colours for his unique costumes while Keith tended towards the more orthodox rock 'n' roll outfit of worn jeans and waistcoat.

Above: Prior to the European tour the band managed to arrange an unpublicized show at the intimate 100 Club at 100 Oxford Street in London. The club is one of the most famous live venues in Europe and has been host to a diverse repertoire of acts since it opened in 1942.

Performing at Wembley

Opposite and right: The tumultuous trio of Ronnie, Keith and Mick perform at Wembley in June 1982.

After his split from Anita Pallenberg, Keith embarked on a steady relationship with American model Patti Hansen. He had met her at his birthday party in 1979 and they soon became an item. They married on 18 December 1983, Keith's 40th Birthday. They had two daughters, Theodora and Alexandra.

The Stones had released their live album, *Still Life (American Concert 1981)*, to coincide with their European Tour. The LP had been recorded during the 1981 American tour and was widely denounced for being too slick, with none of the rough edges usually associated with the band. Nevertheless it was yet another success on both sides of the Atlantic.

European tour winds up

Opposite and left: The triumphant tour closed in front of around 80,000 fans at Roundhay Park in Leeds on 25 July, the night before Mick's 39th birthday. The previous evening the band had played to another huge crowd at the stunning Slane Castle, Ireland, on a picturesque site near the River Boyne.

As the tour came to an end the band's thoughts turned to future projects and a few months later work started on what was to be the next Stones LP, *Undercover*. The hard-rock album consisted of all newly recorded material and was released in November 1983. This was a time when the feuding between the Glimmer Twins was increasing and the friction between them led to further deterioration within their relationship and disillusionment among the other band members.

Something to celebrate

Opposite: Jerry and Mick smile for the cameras as they attend the Berkeley Square Ball in London in July 1984.

Right: Bill Wyman poses with Cilla Black at the party to celebrate the 1000th episode of the long-running TV programme *Top of the Pops* in May 1983. The extended party edition of the programme included many old and new performances including the Stones' popular track "Brown Sugar". The episode also coincided with the first stereo broadcast on BBC Radio 1 so the show was simultaneously broadcast on radio and TV, enabling viewers to listen in stereo.

Solo album for Mick

Opposite: Mick released his debut solo album, *She's the Boss*, in February 1985. This caused further antagonism within the band as they were simultaneously trying to put together The Stones' next album, *Dirty Work*. The other members resented the fact that Mick was putting all his efforts into material for his solo work and not giving enough attention to their joint undertaking.

Right: Looking dapper at the airport, the proud father was eager to return to the UK to show off his new daughter to her paternal grandparents following the birth of Elizabeth Scarlett in March in New York. July 1984 would see the release of the album, *Rewind (1971–1984)* – a retrospective of the previous 13 years. The UK and US editions of the album featured different track listings, reflecting the individual tastes of the two markets.

A third daughter for Mick

Above: Mick has a twinkle in his eye at the christening of daughter, Elizabeth Scarlett on 24 June 1984. The three-month-old baby was christened at the parish church near Mick and Jerry's rented London home. He already had two daughters: 12-year-old Jade, by ex-wife Bianca, and 13-year-old Karis, by American singer Marsha Hunt.

Opposite: The doting dad proudly shows off his baby daughter to the cameras. Despite looking tired he was happy to boast that Elizabeth has "Jerry's sweet disposition and my extravagant good looks"!

Passion for jazz

Opposite: Elegantly attired, as ever, Charlie is pictured in October 1984. He had been involved in several jazz-oriented albums and steadfastly pursued his passion for jazz, taking every opportunity to play in a variety of settings.

Right: Bill leaves Los Angeles in January 1984. His many hobbies and interests include archaeology and he is fascinated by memorabilia. Like Mick, he is also an avid cricket fan and has played in celebrity matches against former England XIs and is involved with the charity cricket team, the Bunburys.

Dancing in the Street

Opposite: David Bowie helps his friends celebrate Jerry's birthday at London's Langan's Brasserrie. He was soon to collaborate on the single "Dancing in the Street" as part of the Live Aid charity event. The original plan was to play the song live in two cities, with Bowie performing in London while Jagger simultaneously sang in Philadelphia. However, the satellite link would have meant there was a time difference of about half a second. Another solution was needed and the pair eventually shot a video together which was shown at both venues during the Live Aid concert in July 1985. When the single was released in August it shot straight to number 1 in the UK charts. Reflecting the fractured state of the band at the time, the five Stones did not play together at the Live Aid concert. Mick performed a solo, backed by Hall and Oates and also appeared with Tina Turner, while Keith and Ronnie played with Bob Dylan.

Above: Ronnie and Charlie smile cheerfully for the camera but both Keith and Mick are more reserved.

Bill supports his favourite charities

Opposite: During the 1980s Bill became very active in fund-raising activities. He is pictured here with Andy Fairweather Low who helped the bassist organize a charity show to support multiple sclerosis research. Following on from Live Aid the pair worked with fellow musicians Chris Rea and Kenny Jones using the name "Hearing Aid".

Right: Mick leaves his London home on 31 October 1985. His first son, James Leroy Augustine, had been born on 28 August 1985 in New York. The christening took place three months later at St Mary Abbot's Church in Kensington.

Supporting Charlie

Above: Keith and Mick in animated conversation at Ronnie Scott's jazz club in London where they had gone to support Charlie. Relations between the two were particularly strained at this time. Keith felt that Mick should prioritize his commitment to the Stones above his solo career and was infuriated that work on his *She's the Boss* album was consuming so much of the singer's time.

Opposite: An impeccably dressed Charlie joins fellow Stones at their reserved table. The jazz-mad drummer was able to fulfil a long-held ambition to play with top jazz musicians when he played at Britain's leading jazz club, Ronnie Scott's, in London on 18 November 1985.

Commemorating Ian Stewart

Opposite: Ronnie, new wife Jo and their two-year-old son Tyrone leave for New York to work on the band's latest album, *Dirty Work*, in March 1986. Ronnie often acted as arbitrator in the bitter arguments between Mick and Keith. When *Dirty Work* was released it was dedicated to one of the founding members of the Stones, Ian Stewart, who had died suddenly of a heart attack at the age of 47.

Above: Bill sits with girlfriend Mandy Smith. He had first met the teenager in February 1984 at an awards ceremony when the aspiring model and actress was only 13 years old. The unlikely liaison gave rise to considerable media attention but did not stop Bill from embarking on a long-term relationship with her.

Mick escorts Karis

Left: Mick escorts his eldest daughter, 16-year-old Karis, on a trip to Barbados for Christmas in December 1986. Despite the lawsuit brought by Marsha Hunt when Karis was two years old, Mick bore no ill will and remained close to his daughter; he attended her graduation from Yale and her wedding in 2000 and was at the hospital in 2004 when her son was born.

Opposite: Bill takes American model Nike Clark to Langan's Brasserie before the couple go on to the exclusive Tramp nightclub early in 1987. His relationship with Mandy Smith had been waning since August 1986. However, it was not the end of the road as their affair was later re-kindled and the couple would marry in 1989.

Primitive Cool

Right: Mick travels to New York in April 1987 to work on his second solo album *Primitive Cool*. Relations between Mick and Keith soured further when Mick decided his project would take precedence over any Stones commitments. The album was a more reflective piece of work than his debut offering, *She's the Boss*, and was co-produced with Eurythmics guitarist Dave Stewart.

Opposite: Jerry and Mick relax on the beach in Barbados in January 1987. Jerry once famously claimed to practise a pearl of wisdom passed on by her mother: "To be a good wife you've got to be a maid in the living room, a cook in the kitchen and a whore in the bedroom."

The quiet life

Above: Charlie lives a quiet life compared with his fellow Stones. Here he is pictured browsing through the cricket memorabilia at the leading art auction house Christies in April 1987.

Opposite: Mick dancing the night away at a party in June 1987 at Knightsbridge restaurant, San Lorenzo. Fellow band member, Ronnie Wood was soon to open his own nightclub in Miami, "Woody's on the Beach", designed by Biba's Barbara Hulanicki.

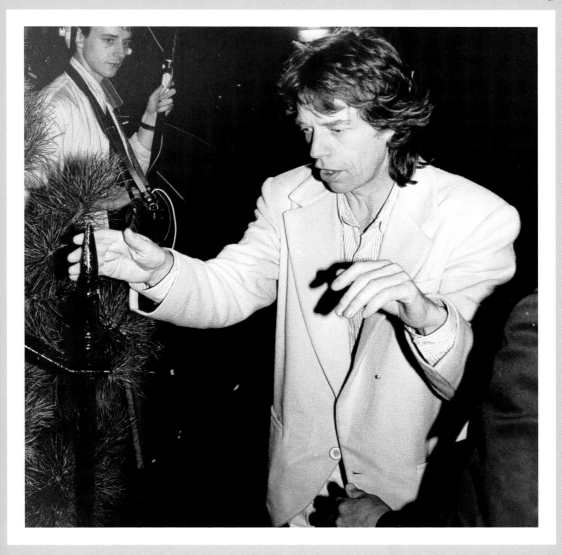

"Let's Work"
Right and opposite: The lead single "Let's Work" from parent album *Primitive Cool* was released prior to the LP, hitting the shops in September 1987. Mick made a live appearance on BBC's *Top of the Pops* on 24 September to promote the song, but it was only a minor hit.

While Mick was busy compiling his solo album, Keith was involved in a documentary about Chuck Berry in honour of Berry's 60th birthday. The film *Hail! Hail! Rock 'n' Roll* chronicled two special performances from the pioneer of the musical genre that so influenced the lead guitarist. Keith also formed a band named the X-Pensive Winos with American songwriter and producer, Steve Jordan.

Artistic expression

Opposite: Ronnie had been born into a musical and artistic family. Before beginning his musical career he had attended Ealing College of Art in London and has been painting and drawing since he was young. He has a reputation as an accomplished artist.

Decades was an exhibition of his paintings and pictures of musicians which opened in London and later transferred to the States. As his musical career progressed, Ronnie continued to paint and draw not only fellow artists, but also family, close friends and self-portraits.

Left: Although the band's touring schedule was quite sparse in the 1980s, Mick completed a tour of Japan where he reportedly received £1 million for each show.

Meanwhile, teaming up again with Steve Jordan, Keith released his own solo album, *Talk is Cheap*, in October 1988 and received some warm reviews. This album also spawned a brief US tour – only one of two that Keith has done as a solo artist.

Bill weds Mandy

Above: Actress Barbara Bach, Ringo Starr's wife, poses with Mandy Smith, Bill Wyman and Jo and Ronnie Wood in May 1989 at the opening of Bill's latest venture – his rock 'n' roll themed restaurant, Sticky Fingers. By this time the rift between Mick and Keith had been healed after the pair had flown to Barbados in January to discuss the future of the band.

Opposite: Bill kisses the cheek of his new bride after the blessing at St John the Evangelist church in London in June 1989. The couple had been married officially in a secret civil ceremony at Bury St Edmunds a few days earlier. The three bridesmaids and page were all cousins of 18-year-old Amanda Louise Wyman, nee Smith. There was a party for more than 500 guests following the ceremony.

Enjoying a drink

Above: A few days after their marriage the happy couple enjoy a drink outside Bill's Sticky Fingers restaurant. Their marriage was to be short-lived and the unlikely pair were divorced two years later.

Opposite: Keith and 19-year-old son Marlon at the Hard Rock Cafe in London in June 1989. Marlon, who had been named after the actor Marlon Brando, grew up in the States where he attended a Quaker school. He married model Lucie de la Falaise in Italy in 1994 and the couple now have two children.

Steel Wheels

Above and opposite: The opening night of the Steel Wheels world tour at the Veterans Stadium, Philadelphia, on 31 August 1989 – the first time the band had been on the road together since the European tour of 1982. The demand for tickets was enormous and advance sales had broken all records. The set for the tour was a diverse mix of classics and new songs which attempted to feature every period of the band's career, and included the use of synthesizers and a full brass band. The unconventional set was designed to resemble a decaying industrial world through the use of scaffolding.

"Mixed Emotions"
Right: Keith on stage. "Mixed Emotions", the single released from the tour album Steel Wheels, was a Jagger-Richards collaboration written during their time in Barbados in January 1989. The lyrics reflected much of the resentment and bitterness that had so dominated their relationship during the 1980s. The song only reached number 35 in the UK charts but fared better in the US where it peaked at number 5.

Opposite: Mick was given round-the-clock protection while on the Steel Wheels tour in America as he was still receiving personal threats nearly 20 years after the Altamont tragedy.

Bill's last album

Left: The massive worldwide Steel Wheels tour was launched in August 1989 with the release of an album of the same name. Recording had started in the spring of the same year in Montserrat and London and heralded the return to a more classic style of music. It was to be the last Rolling Stones album that guitarist Bill Wyman would play on.

Opposite: The New York concert was held at baseball's Shea Stadium when more than 70,000 fans strained to see the Stones' charismatic lead vocalist perform. Steel Wheels was to become the most financially successful rock tour in history up to that time.

Steel Wheels becomes Urban Jungle

Opposite and left: The Steel Wheels tour was revamped as the Urban Jungle European Tour and launched in May 1990. It was to feature a new stage set, designed so that it was easier to move around, as well as a different running order from the original shows.

The tour opened in Rotterdam on 18 May 1990 and finished at Wembley three months later. The emphasis of the shows had changed from the American tour and was more reliant on the type of jokey props which had been used in the 1975 Tour of the Americas. At this Wembley gig on 4 July gigantic inflatable dolls appeared when "Honky Tonk Women" was belted out and blow-up toothy dogs were unleashed during "Street Fighting Man".

First trip to Japan

Left: Mick enhanced the sense of theatre through his many costume changes and use of visual effects. Before the launch of the European tour and after the success in America, the band had taken the Steel Wheels Tour to Japan in February 1990, the first time The Rolling Stones had played there. Their 10 dates at the Tokyo Dome were sold out as the Sports Stadium was transformed into a bleak, monochrome landscape.

Opposite: Keith and Ronnie on stage during the Urban Jungle Tour. The 120,000 tickets for the series of three Wembley shows in July sold out in less than a day as demand once again outstripped supply. The tour was an enormous financial success and it was rumoured that the band members had each grossed £10 million.

Accolades all round

Above: Mick on stage. In March 1990 *Rolling Stone* magazine nominated the band's *Steel Wheels* album for a number of awards including the prestigious best album. The lead single from the album, "Mixed Emotions", was nominated as best single. There were a host of personal nominations for Mick (best male singer), Bill (best bassist) and Charlie (best drummer) as well as accolades for the whole band as best band and artists of 1989.

Opposite: Mick performs for the first time in the Czech Republic on 18 August. The Stones visited President Vaclav Havel in Prague and then performed at the city's Strahov Stadium in front of more than 100,000 people. Posters in the city read "Tanks are rolling out, The Stones are rolling in".

Stone Alone
Left: Bill holds up a copy of his autobiography *Stone Alone (The Story of a Rock 'n' Roll Band)*. The memoir, covering the years prior to 1969, had been launched at his Sticky Fingers restaurant on 24 October 1990 – Bill's 54th birthday.
Opposite: The "Stone Alone" looks happy as he attends a charity ball at The Royal Albert Hall on 12 March 1991. By this time his marriage to Mandy Smith was on the rocks and they would divorce in November the following year. He did not remain single for long, however, marrying fashion designer Suzanne Accosta some five months later.

From one Charlie...

Opposite: The enigmatic drummer re-launched his tribute to Charlie Parker, *Ode to a High Flying Bird*, at Ronnie Scott's Jazz Club on 3 April 1991. Throughout his career he had derived inspiration from the iconic jazz saxophonist; the Charlie Watts Quintet released two records to honour his hero, *From One Charlie* in February 1991 and *Tribute to Charlie Parker with Strings* in August 1992.

Right: Mick and Jerry display their togetherness on their way to Nice in 1991. The couple had married in a Hindu beach ceremony in Bali on 21 November 1990. The Rolling Stones frontman would later claim that that the ceremony was not legally binding and the marriage was annulled nine years later.

Ivor Novello winners

Opposite: Bill and Ronnie proudly show off their trophies after receiving a career Ivor Novello Award on behalf of the band in London on 2 May 1991. The group received the prestigious honour in recognition of their outstanding contribution to British music.

Right: Mick arrives back in Britain from Los Angeles to prepare for National Music day on 29 June 1992. He had been instrumental in initiating the event in order to celebrate a wide range of music. A few days before the occasion Mick and Jerry's second daughter, Georgia May, was christened in Surrey. Charlie Watts was one of the godparents.

Guitar legends

Opposite: Keith performs at the Guitar Legends festival in Seville, Spain, along with Bob Dylan in October 1991. Earlier in the year the Stones had released the live album, *Flashpoint*, the first live album by the group since 1982's *Still Life (American Concert 1981)*. It had been recorded throughout the Steel Wheels/Urban Jungle tours in 1989 and 1990.

Left: National Music Day was made up of about 1,500 events around Britain. Many thousands watched a diverse group of artists ranging from singers Cliff Richard and Jose Carreras to the more rock 'n' roll musicians like Eric Clapton and Mick Jagger.

Celebration of the Blues

Above: Mick performs at the Celebration of the Blues concert at the Hammersmith Odeon in London, his first solo concert for two years. Throughout much of 1992 Mick worked in LA on his third solo album *Wandering Spirit*, released in February 1993. The album was a top 20 hit on both sides of the Atlantic and many critics believe it to be his best solo work.

Opposite: Ronnie Wood was another enthusiastic participant in the Celebration of the Blues concert. He was soon to release his fifth solo album, *Slide on This*. The LP had been partially recorded in Dublin, where U2's iconic guitarist the Edge featured as a guest musician, but it was not a commercial success.

Duet with a Blues legend

Opposite: Mick sings a duet with Blues legend Jimmie Rogers at the Celebration of the Blues event. Other performers on the night included the Charlie Watts Quintet, Ronnie Wood and Buddy Guy. Charlie and Ronnie joined Mick for a rendition of "I Just Want to Make Love to You".

Above: The musical maestro acknowledges the contributions of the performers who had participated in the day. Although 1982 was a sparse year for the group overall, it was a productive year for solo Stones; along with Mick's and Ronnie's works, Keith also released an album. *Main Offender*, his second solo offering, was a collaboration with his other band, The X-Pensive-Winos.

Ronnie's solo ventures

Opposite: Ronnie and Jo Wood with children 13-year-old Leah and 9-year-old Tyrone. The couple had married in 1985 in Denham, Hertfordshire. In January 1993 Ronnie embarked on a series of concerts in North America and Japan to promote his solo album *Slide On This*. This later resulted in the release of his first live LP, a spin-off of the original album, *Slide On Live: Plugged In and Standing*.

Above: A pensive Bill Wyman as he is chauffeured to his divorce proceeding. His marriage to Mandy had been in difficulties for some time, partly due to the guitarists extended absences in America and Mandy's health problems. The divorce was finalized in November 1992 and both parties soon found consolation with others.

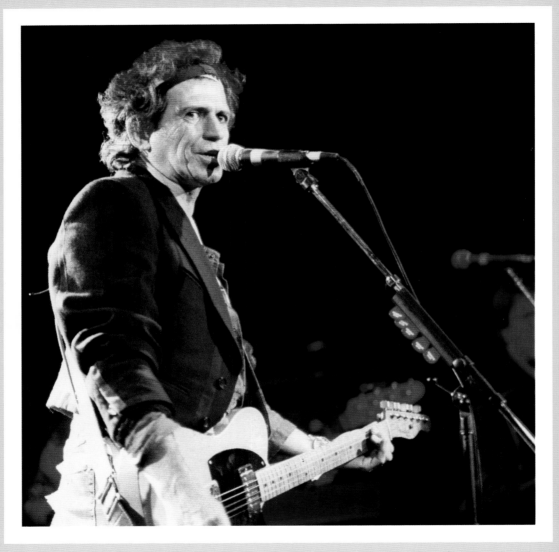

Keith's X-Pensive Winos

Opposite: Keith flies solo at London's Marquee Club in December 1992. He was in the middle of a month-long European tour with The X-Pensive Winos. His band would soon jet off to the States for their imminent American tour in January 1993.

Above: Ronnie with his daughter Leah and Paul Young at the Brit Awards in February 1993. Ronnie and Bill were filling in for the ailing Ronnie Lane in a Faces re-union to celebrate Rod Stewart's outstanding contribution award.

Bill announces his retirement

Left: Bill plays at The Brit Awards at Alexandra Palace in London. On 6 January he appeared on the TV programme *London Tonight* and announced that he was finally leaving the band saying, "I really don't want to do it anymore. I have many special memories. It's been wonderful. But I thought the last two tours with them were the best we have ever done, so I was quite happy to stop after that." He now continues to tour with his blues rock band, The Rhythm Kings, formed in 1997.

Opposite: A relaxed-looking Mick in April 1993. Together with song-writing partner Keith Richards he was soon to be inducted into the songwriters' Hall of Fame –an organization which honours celebrated musicians who have made rock and roll the force that it is in our culture. The band as an entity had already been inducted in 1989.

Time to relax for Bill
Opposite: Bill celebrates his fourth wedding anniversary with wife Suzanne Accosta at his Sticky Fingers restaurant in 1997. The couple have three daughters: Katherine, Jessica and Matilda, born in 1994, 1995 and 1998 respectively.
Right: Rain stopped play but the former Stone remains relaxed at one of his charity cricket matches in June 1993. With no Stones commitments and more time on his hands Bill Wyman had more time to pursue his own hobbies and interests.

Time for some r'n'r before the next tour

Right: The ever-ebullient Ronnie enjoys a tipple at a celebrity party hosted by comedians Peter Cook and Dudley Moore. The four remaining band members were able to enjoy a more relaxed lifestyle between the end of their Urban Jungle tour in August 1990 and the beginning of Voodoo Lounge four years later.

Opposite: Mick leaves Quaglino's restaurant in London amidst preparations for the forthcoming Voodoo Lounge Tour in August 1994. The mammoth year-long tour covered five continents, starting in North American and ending in Europe.

Darryl Jones stands in for Wyman

Left: Guns 'n' Roses guitarist Slash helps Ronnie celebrate his 47th birthday on 1 June 1994, while legendary guitarist Eric Clapton joins in the festivities with the Woods (opposite). Preparations for the Voodoo Lounge Tour were well under way by this time. The supporting album was released in July and was the first to be recorded without bassist Bill Wyman. Although he had not officially joined the band, Chicago-born guitarist Darryl Jones took the founding member's place and now routinely tours and performs with the band. The *Voodoo Lounge* album was released under the Virgin Record label following their new contract with Richard Branson which had been agreed in November 1991. The studio album was generally well received and was the band's first chart topping album in the UK since *Emotional Rescue* in 1980.

Voodoo Lounge Tour

Opposite and above: The Voodoo Lounge Tour opened at the Robert F. Kennedy Memorial Stadium in Washington, DC, on 8 August 1994. Following the success of the Steel Wheels/Urban Jungle stage sets, the latest tour again used a technological approach as the band played in front of a huge Jumbotron screen surrounded by a cobra-shaped tower. Banks of lights and the use of pyrotechnics completed the magnificent spectacle.

The theatrical tour included dates in North and South America, South Africa, Japan, New Zealand and Australia before the final leg in Europe started in May 1995. While the tour was in full swing the album *Voodoo Lounge* won the Grammy Award for Best Rock Album in March 1995.

Jerry calls time

Left: Mick and Jerry attend a fundraiser in May 1995. The couple had always had a mercurial relationship and Jerry was philosophical about Mick's womanizing. However, her tolerance and patience were finally tested to the limit when Brazilian model Luciano Morad gave birth to the straying Stone's son in May 1998. This was one dalliance too many and Jerry finally filed for divorce.

Opposite: Ronnie raises his arm aloft at the open-air Hyde Park concert in 1996. Prince Charles watched as the band joined other distinguished musicians including The Who, Bob Dylan and Eric Clapton who had all donated their services in order to raise money for the Prince's Trust charity.

Ronnie gains recognition

Opposite: Ronnie is surrounded by some of his paintings. He has maintained his love of art throughout his musical career. He is recognized in the art world as an established artist in his own right and in March 2004 appeared with Melvyn Bragg on the *South Bank Show* in a documentary devoted to his work. The acerbic art critic Brian Sewell has also called Wood "an accomplished and respectable artist". He now co-owns a London art gallery called Scream with sons Jamie and Tyrone.

Above: Mick and Jerry attend a theatre awards ceremony in London. Despite the fact that their marriage was annulled in 1999 Mick and Jerry remain good friends and he attended the first night of Jerry's debut playing Mrs Robinson in *The Graduate* in June 2000.

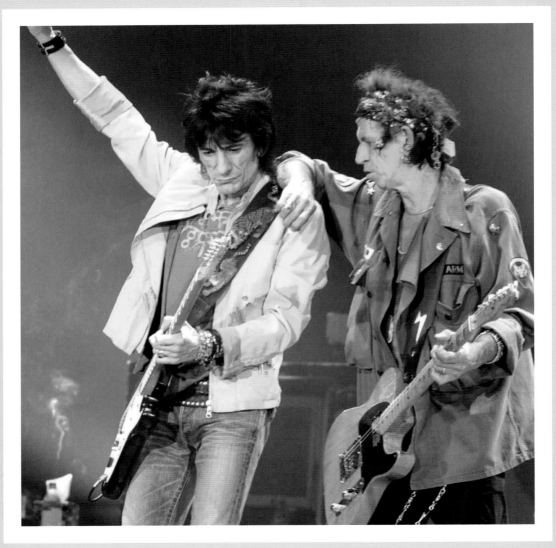

Time is on their side

The first decade of the new millennium was a busy one for the Stones. In 2002 they released *Forty Licks* to mark their fortieth anniversary as a band. The Licks tour of 2002-03 included shows in North America, Europe and Asia and the ensuing double live album *Live Licks* went Gold.

The A Bigger Bang tour, coinciding with the release of the *A Bigger Bang* album, kicked off in Toronto in August 2005 and covered North and South America, Australasia, and Europe, before finishing in London in August 2007.

And so the Stones keep rolling on. The most enduring rock band of all time still can sing "Time is on my side" with the same conviction bestowed on the song back in 1963...

Opposite and right: Ronnie, Keith and Mick performing live onstage, during the Americas leg of the A Bigger Bang tour

Chronology

1936

24 October   Bill Wyman (William Perks) is born in Lewisham, south London.

1941

2 June   Charlie Watts (Charles Robert Watts) is born in Islington, north London.

1942

28 February   Brian Jones (Lewis Brian Hopkin Jones) is born in Cheltenham, Gloucestershire.

1943

26 July   Mick Jagger (Michael Philip Jagger) is born in Dartford, Kent.

18 December   Keith Richards is born in Dartford, Kent.

1947

1 June   Ronnie Wood (Ronald Wood) is born in Hillingdon, Middlesex.

1948

17 January   Mick Taylor (Michael Taylor) is born in Welwyn Garden City, Hertfordshire.

1962

March   Alexis Korner's Blues Incorporated begin regular Saturday night gigs at the Ealing Jazz Club in west London. Mick Jagger and Keith Richards become friends after a chance meeting on a south London train.

April   Mick and Keith meet Brian at the Ealing Club – the idea of forming a band is born. Mick starts singing with Blues Incorporated, sometimes at the Marquee Club in Soho.

May   The band is formed but is not named the Rollin' Stones until June.

12 July   First gig as the Stones at the Marquee. Many more on the London club circuit follow.

December   Bill Wyman considers joining the band, by now called the Rolling Stones.

1963

January   Charlie Watts' recruitment persuades Bill Wyman to enlist with the group. First demo recordings are cut but no record label offers a contract.

April   The Beatles see the band in a Richmond, Surrey club and a friendship is forged while socialising in the Chelsea flat shared by Mick and Keith. Andrew Loog Oldham decides to manage the band.

10 May   Oldham produces the first cut of 'Come On' – destined to become the Stones' first single.

18 May   Journalist Norman Jopling files the first national rave review of the band.

7 June   'Come on/I Wanna Be Loved' is released on Decca, reaching No. 20 in the British charts in August. For their first UK TV appearance the Rolling Stones all wear the same neat clothes. The band continues to perform at small clubs, private parties and halls. More TV appearances follow throughout the summer.

29 September   The Rolling Stones' first tour begins at the Victoria Theatre in London, the band supporting Bo Diddley and the Everly Brothers.

1 November   A second single, 'I Wanna Be Your Man', a Lennon-McCartney composition, is released. It enters the charts on 8 November and remains there for thirteen weeks, reaching No. 9.

28 November   The Stones meet American singer Gene Pitney. Three weeks later his record 'That Girl Belongs to Yesterday', written by Jagger and Richards and produced by Loog Oldham, begins its UK chart ascent.

1964

6 January   The Rolling Stones' second British tour opens in Harrow, north-west London.

17 January   An EP (extended play) is released, featuring five tracks. It spent eleven weeks in the singles charts, reaching No. 15.

8 February   Another UK tour begins in London. It will close on March 7, just as the band's new single 'Not Fade Away', is released in the UK and the US.

16 April   Decca release their first album, *The Rolling Stones*. On 24 April it reaches No. 1 in the British album charts.

1 May   A third UK tour begins, the day before 'Not Fade Away' enters the US charts. The single remains there for 13 weeks but does not achieve a high placing.

19 May   Riots in Hamilton, Scotland, as police attempt to calm 4,000 fans – some with forged tickets – who storm a gig at a local hotel.

1 June   The band fly to New York for their first American tour. More than 5,000 fans greet them at Kennedy airport.

5 June   First US concert in San Bernardino, California. A few days later they fail to fill a stadium in San Antonio, where locals profess to prefer their high school band. However, in other cities over the next few weeks The Stones are greeted rapturously.

23 June   British fans riot at London airport as the band returns.

26 June   'It's All Over Now' is released and enters the British singles charts a week later at No. 7, making No. 1 soon afterwards.

24 July   A new British tour opens in Blackpool. Thirty of the 7,000 fans present, and two policemen, are injured in the crush.

31 July   A concert in Belfast is abandoned after twelve minutes as hysterical girls are lifted away in straight-jackets.

6 August   The Rolling Stones record an appearance for a networked American TV show. The next day they return to their roots and perform at the Richmond Jazz and Blues Festival, and then record for ITV's seminal *Ready, Steady, Go* television programme.

14 August   The EP 'Five by Five' is released by Decca, recorded in Chicago in June. It is in Britain's singles' chart within days.

Aug   Marianne Faithfull's single 'As Tears Go By' is released.

5 September   A new British tour begins at the Finsbury Park Astoria in London.

13 September   Thousands of fans are restrained by rugby players hired as a 'human shield' at a concert in Liverpool.

9 October   The album *12 x 5* is released in the USA, two days before the tour finishes in south London.

14 October   Charlie Watts marries Shirley Ann Shephard in Bradford, Yorkshire.

17 October   'Time Is On My Side' enters the US charts at No. 80. It will remain there for thirteen weeks without becoming a major hit.

18 October   The band is banned from appearing on Belgian TV after 5,000 fans greeted them at the airport in Brussels. Two days later, French fans riot in Paris.

23 October   The Rolling Stones fly to New York for their second US tour.

24 October   Ed Sullivan promises his massive TV show audience that the Stones will never appear again. He professes to be shocked by them.

31 October   After a further series of triumphant and controversial US dates and filming of their slot for the classic film *Gather No Moss*, the Stones greet loyal fans in San Bernardino and go on to many other gigs before the tour ends in November.

20 November   Back in Britain the new single 'Little Red Rooster' goes straight to the top spot in the British charts. The band is simultaneously banned from a BBC radio programme for failing to honour an earlier booking.

21 December   Charlie Watts' book about Charlie Parker, *Ode to a High Flying Bird*, is published.

1965

15 January   *Rolling Stones No. 2*, their second album, is released.

21 January   The group arrive in Sydney, Australia. 3,000 fans welcome them.

22 January   The new album enters British charts at No. 1.

31 January   The Rolling Stones fly to New Zealand after nine sell-out gigs in Melbourne.

17 February   After the final tour date, in Hong Kong, the group flies to the USA.

26 February   'The Last Time' single is released. It will enter the charts at No. 8 and then hold the No. 1 position for four weeks.

5 March   A two-week British tour begins.

18 March   After the tour ends in Romford, Essex, there are complaints when Mick Jagger, Brian Jones and Bill Wyman urinate against a garage forecourt wall.

24 March   The Rolling Stones begin a short Scandinavian tour in Denmark, and go on to West Germany and Paris.

22 April   Start of the the Rolling Stones' third tour of North America.

26 April   The group is forced to leave the stage in London, Ontario, after police turn off the power.

2 May   The Rolling Stones appear again on the Ed Sullivan TV show in New York.

27 May   'Satisfaction' is released in the USA.

30 May   Final date of the tour, in New York. Shortly afterwards, the Rolling Stones beat the Beatles into second place in an American pop poll.

11 June   The EP (extended play) 'Got Live If You Want It' is released.

15 June   Beginning of a short tour of Scotland.

23 June   Start of a Scandinavian tour, opening in Norway.

1 July   It is reported that summonses have been issued against Wyman, Jones and Jagger for their alleged 'insulting behaviour' in Essex on the night of 18 March. On 22 July each would be fined £5.

10 July   Their third album, *Out Of Our Heads*, is about to be released.

1 August   Launch of Andrew Loog Oldham's Immediate record label.

20 August   'Satisfaction' is released in the UK, entering the charts at No. 3 a week later. It will spend three weeks at No. 1.

3 September   The first of several shows in Dublin, Belfast and the Isle of Man, followed by a new tour of West Germany and Austria.

15 September   Fans demolish fifty rows of seats at a hall in West Berlin and then vandalise a train. Four hundred riot police do battle with them. Thirty-two fans and six policemen need hospital treatment.

24 September   Start of a 22-date British tour which coincides with the release of *Out Of Our Heads*.

22 October   The single 'Get Off of My Cloud' is released.

29 October   The Rolling Stones open their fourth North American tour in Montreal.

5 November   'Get Off Of My Cloud' is simultaneously No. 1 in the UK and the USA.

14 November   A new LP, *December's Children*, is released in the USA.

5 December   The tour finishes in San Diego, California.

1966

1 January   *Ready, Steady, Go* TV slot.

4 February   Release of single '19th Nervous Breakdown'.

12 February   The group flies to New York for TV appearances, going on to tour Australia and New Zealand.

1 March   Final tour date in Auckland. Later this month Cliff Richard will release the single 'Blue Turns to Grey', written by Jagger and Richard.

12 March   The last of 21 new tracks are recorded   at the RCA Studios in Hollywood. Many will be included on the forthcoming album, *Aftermath*.

25 March   Beginning of a two-week European tour.

30 March   Fans in Marseilles take on the police as hysteria mounts during a concert. The group's first anthology album, *Big Hits (High Tide and Green Grass)* has been released.

15 April   Release of the classic album *Aftermath*. One track 'Goin' Home' runs for nearly twelve minutes – unprecedented in pop music. The album will spend seven weeks at No. 1 in the British charts. The single 'Paint It Black' is released in the USA this month.

13 May   'Paint It Black' is released in the UK. It will chart for six weeks, reaching No. 1. Keith Richard has bought Redlands, a moated house, in Sussex.

17 June   Chris Farlowe's single 'Out Of Time', written by Jagger and Richards, is released on Immediate Records.

23 June   The Stones arrive in New York for their sell-out fifth North American tour, staying on a chartered yacht in the harbour as so many hotels have declined to take their booking. .

28 July   The tour closes in Hawaii, after which the band record in Hollywood and make TV appearances before taking holidays and returning to Britain.

27 August   Having hurt his hand on holiday in north Africa, it is rumoured that Brian Jones will be unable to play for at least two months.

23 September   'Have You Seen Your Mother Baby, Standing In The Shadow' is released as the Rolling Stones' new single. Its picture sleeve (a novelty) depicts band members in drag and the record is banned by the BBC. Nonetheless it enters the charts a week later, peaking at No. 5.

24 September   Start of a new UK tour.

4 November   The album *Got Live If You Want It* is released in the USA, reaching No. 6 in a chart stay of 48 weeks. This month Brian Jones posed in Nazi regalia with Anita Pallenberg. The band cuts material for a new album in a Paris studio.

December   Mick Jagger and Chrissie Shrimpton part. He is involved with Marianne Faithfull by then. Shrimpton attempted suicide.

1967

13 January   'Let's Spend The Night Together' is released. The single's B-side is the elegiac 'Ruby Tuesday'. Several US radio stations ban the record and Jagger has to sing 'Let's Spend Some Time Together' on an American TV show.

20 January   Release of a new album, *Between The Buttons* – all tracks written by Jagger and Richard.

22 January   The group appear on the family-orientated British TV variety show, *Sunday Night At The London Palladium*, but refuse to join other stars waving on the stage roundabout which traditionally closes the show.

15 February   Fifteen police officers raid Keith Richard's Sussex home armed with a warrant issued under the Dangerous Drugs Act.

Soon Jagger, Jones, Richard and various women friends head for Morocco, hoping to relax after the Sussex 'bust'. On the way, asthmatic Brian Jones is admitted to a French hospital with respiratory problems.

10 March   Brian flies from Nice to hospital in London. By the time he is well enough to join the party in Marrakesh, Anita Pallenberg and Keith Richard have become lovers. Whilst Brian was out recording ethnic music the others flew home from Tangier via Madrid. They left no note.

18 March   Brian returns to London. Jagger and Richard are issued with court summonses.

25 March   A three-week European tour opens in Sweden and will include concerts in West Germany, Austria, Italy, France, Switzerland, Holland and Poland.

10 May   After the first of a series of court appearances relating to the raid at his Sussex home, Keith Richard, and Mick Jagger, are remanded on bail. On the same day Brian Jones is arrested at home in Kensington for separate drug-related offences. He too is given bail.

15 June   Jagger and Richard supply backing vocals for the Beatles' single 'All You Need Is Love'. A new compilation album, *Flowers*, is released this month.

27/28 June   Jagger and Richards' cases are heard at a court in Chichester, West Sussex. They are both given prison sentences and told to pay costs.

30 June   Jagger and Richard are awarded bail and the right of appeal.

31 July   In the court of appeal Mick is given a conditional discharge and Keith Richards' sentence is quashed.

18 August   The single 'We Love You' is released.

26 August   Mick Jagger and Marianne Faithfull join the Beatles at the Maharishi Marhesh Yogi's seminar in Wales.

29 September   The Rolling Stones part company with Andrew Loog Oldham.

30 October   Brian is sentenced to nine months' imprisonment for drug offences. He is released on bail from Wormwood Scrubs the next day and on 12 December his sentence is commuted to three years' probation.

27 November   The album *Their Satanic Majesties Request* is released in the USA. It will be weeks before it is available in Britain.

14 December   *Their Satanic Majesties Request* enters the British album charts and remains there for nine weeks, reaching No. 3. Brian Jones collapses and is rushed to a London hospital suffering from strain and exhaustion.

1968

13 March   The band are in the Olympic Studios in London, cutting a new album, work which will continue until 18 April.

11 May   It is announced that Mick Jagger is to star in a film called *The Performance*.

21 May   Brian Jones is arrested for possession of cannabis at home in Chelsea. He denies the charge.

25 May   The classic single 'Jumpin' Jack Flash' is released. It will reach No. 1 in both the UK and the USA.

26 July   The single 'Street Fighting Man', taken from the Stones' forthcoming album, is released in the USA.

24 August   Disputes about the 'lavatorial' sleeve of the new album delay *Beggars' Banquet*'s release.

3 September   'Street Fighting Man' is banned in Chicago after political demonstrations.

12 September   As Mick Jagger begins work on his film, now called *Performance*.

26 September   In a London court Brian Jones is fined for possession of cannabis.

4 October   Marianne Faithful happily announces her pregnancy. Six weeks later and nearly six months pregnant she loses her baby.

21 November   Brian Jones buys Cotchford Farm in Sussex, formerly the home of A.A. Milne, creator of Winnie the Pooh.

5 December   *Beggars' Banquet* is at last released in Britain, with an ironic sleeve spoofing an invitation to a formal party. It enters the charts days later, at No. 3 and remains there for twelve weeks without going higher.

1969

March   The band return to Olympic Studios in London to cut a new album. Jagger and Richard work together on new songs, spending time writing in Italy in April.

28 May   After a police raid at Jagger's Chelsea home, he and Marianne are arrested for possession of cannabis. They are remanded and released on bail.

8 June   Band members collect at Cotchford Farm and an amicable split is agreed with Brian Jones. Musical differences are cited.

10 June   Mick Taylor is appointed as Jones' replacement.

1 July   Drug charges against Mick Jagger and Marianne Faithful are adjourned until 29 September.

2/3 July   The body of Brian Jones is lifted from the bottom of his swimming pool at Cotchford Farm. A coroner later reports that he had drowned under the influence of alcohol and drugs.

5 July   A free Rolling Stones concert in London's Hyde Park goes ahead as planned. Thousands of white butterflies are released as Mick Jagger reads from Shelley in Brian's honour.

8 July   Marianne Faithfull overdoses and falls into a long coma in Australia. Another actor takes over her part in *Ned Kelly*. 'Honky Tonk Women' enters the US and UK charts. Two weeks later it will be No. 1 in Britain.

9 July   The divorce of Bill and Diane Wyman is announced.

10 July   Brian Jones is buried in Cheltenham.

13 July   Mick Jagger starts work on *Ned Kelly*. Filming ends in September.

12 September   Another compilation album, *Through The Past Darkly (Big Hits Volume 2)* is released. It reaches No. 1 and will stay in the British charts for sixteen weeks.

17 October   The Rolling Stones fly to Los Angeles to prepare for their first American tour in three years and to mix the next album, *Let It Bleed*. It will be released in Britain in December.

7 November   This sixth American tour is a sell-out and opens in Colorado.

13 November   Warner Bros waver about the US release of *Performance* because they find the English actors' accents 'unintelligible'.

28 November   *Let It Bleed* goes on sale in the USA and the Rolling Stones are triumphant at a filmed Madison Square Garden concert.

6 December   At Altamont, California, the final concert of the tour descends into tragedy. Three fans die and many more are seriously injured.

19 December   At a London court Mick Jagger is fined for possession of cannabis. Marianne Faithfull is acquitted.

21 December   The band give two Christmas shows at a ballroom off the Strand, London.

1970

31 July   The Rolling Stones' contract with Decca expires. The band are set to launch their own record label.

6 September   Release of the *Get Yer Ya Yas Out!* album which reaches No. 1 and remains in the charts for thirteen weeks.

10 October   The day before the European tour ends in Munich, Mick Jagger visits London with a new girlfriend, the Nicaraguan Bianca Perez Morena de Macia.

20 October   Mick Jagger, cited as co-respondent, is ordered to pay costs in John Dunbar's divorce from Marianne Faithfull.

6 December   A documentary film, *Gimme Shelter*, covering the Stones' last American tour and featuring scenes from Altamont, is premiered in New York.

1971

4 January   British premier of *Performance*.

6 February   A farewell tour is announced amidst expectations that the band will become tax exiles in France. It opens in Newcastle and ends at the Roundhouse in north London.

26 March   The Rolling Stones are filmed in performance for TV at the Marquee Club.

1 April   The band gives a farewell party in Maidenhead before leaving for France. Band members take up residence in different but neighbouring houses.

15 April   'Brown Sugar' the Stones' next single, is featured on the BBC's *Top of the Pops*. It enters the charts a week later and will reach No. 1.

23 April   Release of the *Sticky Fingers* LP.

12 May   Mick Jagger marries Bianca in a civil ceremony in St Tropez. Both wear white suits. The bride is already several months pregnant.

28 May   Keith Richard has a road accident and will appear in court on subsequent assault charges. *Gimme Shelter* is screened in Cannes.

1 June   The Rolling Stones top the British singles and album charts with 'Brown Sugar' and *Sticky Fingers*.

31 July   British premier of *Gimme Shelter*.

31 August   The four surviving original Stones and Brian Jones' father launch a complex law suit against Andrew Loog Oldham about alleged irregularities relating to earnings derived through their original recording contract with Decca and other rights.

October   The mixing of twenty new recorded songs continues and the band plans a new album to coincide with next spring's American tour.

December   The band work on the new album at the Sunset Sound studios in Los Angeles. .

3 December   French magistrates accept Keith Richards' defence of self defence after the 'assault' that followed his road accident in May. Charges are dismissed.

15 December   Decca release a double compilation album, *Hot Rocks 1964–1971*.

1972

20 February   Decca release another anthology album, *Milestones*.

14 April   Release of single 'Tumbling Dice' a track from the forthcoming *Exile On Main Street* album. It will reach No. 5 in the British charts.

26 May   *Exile On Main Street*, a double album, is released by Rolling Stones Records.

3 June   The seventh North American tour opens in Vancouver. Thirty policemen are injured as 2,000 fans attempt to gatecrash.

31 July   The marathon tour finishes in New York on Mick Jagger's birthday.

20 November   Mick Jagger sings back-up on Carly Simon's single 'You're So Vain'.

25 November   Band members convene in Kingston, Jamaica for four weeks' recording.

23 December   An earthquake devastates Nicaragua. After Christmas Mick and Bianca Jagger fly there to search for her family and bring medicines. A benefit concert for victims of the earthquake is announced in the new year. Various fund-raising activities eventually raise £350,000.

1973

8 January   Mick's hopes to play in Japan are dashed as an old drugs conviction prevents his entry. A tour has to be cancelled despite record-breaking ticket sales.

21/22 January   The Rolling Stones preview their Australasian tour with two concerts in Honolulu.

March   The new album is mixed in Los Angeles.

18 June   Marsha Hunt files an application at a London court, claiming Mick Jagger is her daughter Karis's father. The court orders that blood tests are taken.

26 June   Keith Richard and two others are arrested in Chelsea for possession of cannabis. Keith is also charged with possessing a firearm and ammunition without a license. He is remanded on bail.

20 August   'Angie', recorded in Jamaica is released and will chart at No. 2. Both the single and the album it was cut from will be No. 1 in the USA in October.

31 August   *Goats Head Soup* is released and will hold the No. 1 position for two weeks.

1 September   The European tour opens in Mannheim, West Germany.

7 September   First British leg of the tour at Wembley – one of four dates there.

17 September   Final British show in Birmingham. The tour continues with concerts in Germany, Holland, Belgium and Scandinavia, closing in Berlin on 19 October.

24 October   Keith Richard is fined £205 for possession of various drugs, firearms and ammunition. For her possession of Mandrax, Anita Pallenberg is conditionally discharged.

13 November   The Rolling Stones begin new recording sessions in Munich.

1974

5 January   Bill Wyman is in Los Angeles recording a solo album. *Monkey Grip* will be released in May on the Rolling Stones' own label.

1 March   A film about their US tour, *Ladies and Gentlemen, The Rolling Stones* is previewed in New York.

9 July   The Rolling Stones preview 'It's Only Rock 'n' Roll (But I like It)' on BBC TV's Old Grey Whistle Test. The single hit the charts on 30 July, making No. 10.

7 December   The band embark on new recording in Munich.

12 December   It is announced that Mick Taylor is leaving the band. In the first place he will work with former Cream bassist Jack Bruce. Massive speculation about his replacement centres on the possibility of Ronnie Wood of the Faces joining them.

31 December   Ronnie Wood insists that his commitment remains with the Faces.

1975

9 February   After recording in Rotterdam Mick Jagger flies to New York whilst Keith Richard returns to London and works with Ronnie Wood at the latter's home studio in Richmond.

22 March   Recording sessions continue in Munich where the band is soon joined by Ronnie Wood.

14 April   It is announced that Ronnie Wood will join the Stones for part of their new American tour, but merely 'guesting' and on loan from the Faces.

1 May   New York is brought to a standstill as the Rolling Stones perform 'Brown Sugar' from the back of a truck. The tour as planned will be the band's longest ever.

13 May   Ronnie Wood departs to join the Faces for their overlapping tour.

13 June   Mid-tour the band release a compilation album, *Made In The Shade*, on their own label.

5 July   Keith Richard, travelling with Ronnie Wood,is arrested on the highway in Fordyce, Arkansas, charged with possession of an offensive weapon – a tin-opener with a blade attachment. Both are released on bail.

August   The South American shows having been postponed, the tour closes in Buffalo.

13 October   The Rolling Stones and Ronnie Wood begin recording new album material at studios in Montreux. Sessions there finish on 15 November.

3 December   Further recording continues in Munich until 16 December.

18 December   As Rod Stewart quits the Faces, apparently unhappy about Ronnie Wood's frequent 'borrowings' by the Stones, rumours that Ronnie will become an official Stone strengthen.

1976

26 February   Release of *Stone Alone*, Bill Wyman's solo album.

20 April   Release of the album *Black And Blue*. It enters the British charts a week later and reaches No. 2.

28 April   The tour opens in Frankfurt.

8 May   'Fool To Cry' enters the British singles charts. It will reach No. 4.

10 May   The British tour begins with a show in Glasgow.

19 May   After crashing his Bentley in Buckinghamshire police find 'substances' in the wreckage. Richard was astonished to learn later that the substances were LSD and cocaine and some newspapers speculated that a Rolling Stone could be used as an unwitting drugs courier.

4 June   Just before going onstage at the Abattoirs for the first of three concerts in Paris, Keith Richard learns that his ten-week-old son Tara has died of a mysterious virus. White and stricken he played on, and insisted that the tragedy should remain secret and that tour plans should not be disrupted.

23 August   The band performs before 200,000 fans, headlining the Knebworth Festival.

September   Mick and Ronnie Wood have whittled down 150 hours of live concert tapes for a new live LP.

6 October   Before a magistrate Keith Richard chooses to go to a higher court for his recent charges to be heard. Bail is renewed at £5,000.

1977

12 January   At Aylesbury Crown Court, after a three day trial with Mick lending supportive presence, Keith is found guilty of possessing cocaine. He is fined £750 and ordered to pay £250 costs. The following month he is fined a further £25 for driving without tax on the night of the accident the previous May.

February   At Toronto airport Anita Pallenberg is arrested, then released. Days later both are charged with possession of

heroin but released, Keith on bail. A court hearing is eventually set for March 14 when Anita is fined $400. For his alleged crimes Keith is remanded on bail.

15 May   Touring in Britain Nils Lofgren dedicates his song 'Keith Don't Go (To Toronto)' to Richard whose voluntary treatment for drug addiction renders him unable to attend a Toronto court appearance. It is rescheduled for 19 July when he is once again unable to appear. The case is adjourned to December.

13 September   The live album which will reach No. 3 in the British charts, *Love You Live* is launched at the Marquee Club in London. Keith cannot attend.

23 September   The film of the band in concert, *Ladies And Gentlemen, The Rolling Stones* is premiered at the Rainbow Theatre in London. The band will soon begin to record a new album in Paris, resuming work on 5 December after a break.

19 November   A compilation album, *Get Stoned*, is released and sells well.

26 November   Mick Jagger goes to Morocco with Jerry Hall, with whom he will fly to Barbados after Christmas in London together.

1978

19 March   Krissie Wood files for divorce, citing model Jo Howard in her petition.

14 May   Bianca Jagger files for divorce in London.

19 May   'Miss You' is released. It reaches No. 2 in the British charts.

9 June   The *Some Girls* album is released the day before their American tour opens in Florida. 55,000 tickets for the 10 July gig at Anaheim, California sell out within two hours. More than $1,000,000 is taken in advance sales for the 80,000 capacity auditorium in New Orleans where the band play on 13 July.

26 July   The tour ends at Oakland, California.

20 October   As of now, Keith is once again Keith Richards.

23 October   Keith Richards' trial in Toronto starts at last. He is given a one year suspended prison sentence and ordered to give a charity concert. People incensed by the judge's leniency will begin an appeal for a harsher sentence the following month.

3 December   Keith's first solo single, 'Run Rudolph Run' is released in the USA. The UK release in February misses the Christmas rush.

15 December   Japan relents after six years and lifts its ban on the Rolling Stones.

1979

18 January   The band convenes in Nassau to cut new album material.

21 April   The Rolling Stones give their only live performance of the year in Toronto, arranged by Keith Richards to meet his recent sentencing stipulation.

18 June   The band gathers in Paris to cut a new album. Work will continue intermittently for some months.

27 June   Keith Richards' appeal case is heard in Toronto. No decision was made as to whether he should, after all, be jailed.

17 September   A Canadian court finally rejects the appeal against Keith Richards' light sentence.

19 October   Paris recordings finish. It is planned to release the new album in January.

2 November   Bianca is granted a decree nisi and custody of daughter Jade.

18 December   At his birthday party in New York Keith Richards meets American model Patti Hansen, whom he will eventually marry.

1980

20 June   The single 'Emotional Rescue', taken from the forthcoming album of the same name, is released. It will reach No. 1 and stay there for four weeks. The next single, 'She's So Cold' is released in September but is less successful.

11 October   Recording sessions for a new album begin in Paris.

2 November   At a private hearing at the High Court in London, Bianca Jagger's divorce settlement is adjudged. It is thought to be in the region of £1,000,000.

1981

January   Mick Jagger flies to Peru with Jerry Hall. He is to star in the Werner Herzog film *Fitzcarraldo* but leaves the project the following month.

4 March   The anthology LP, *Sucking In The Seventies* is produced by Mick and Keith and released on the Rolling Stones' label. It will be released in the UK on 13 April.

July   Bill Wyman's solo single 'Je Suis Un Rock Star' is released and reaches No. 11 in the British charts.

17 August   'Start Me Up', produced by Mick and Keith, is released, taken from the forthcoming *Tattoo You* album. It will sell a million copies in the US in the week of its early September release.

25 September   The tour opens in Philadelphia before a 90,000 strong crowd.

19 December   Another tour finishes in Virginia. It is estimated that the band grossed $50 million in ticket sales and earned almost half as much again via merchandising, record sales and sponsorship. A film of the fifty-date tour has been shot by Hal Ashby for release in 1982.

1982

11 January   'Hang Fire' is released in the US.

26 April   The band's first British concert for six years – in Aberdeen. European tour dates are arranged.

June   Sell-out concerts in London and Bristol. The tour finishes at Leeds.

1 June   A live album, *Still Life*, is released.

24 June   On behalf of the band Bill Wyman collects the British Music Industry's award for outstanding achievement.

September   Another single from the *Still Life* album, 'Time Is On My Side', is released in the USA. In Britain the song is issued as part of a 12-inch single featuring two other songs.

7 November   Recording sessions resume at the Paris studios.

November   A double anthology album, *The Best Of The Rolling Stones*, is released this month on a budget label.

1983

14 January   Mick Jagger plays the Chinese Emperor in a US TV production of *The Nightingale* by Hans Christian Andersen.

25 August   The Rolling Stones sign with CBS in a $28,000,000 deal said to make music business history. Later in August it is announced that Jerry Hall is pregnant and that Bill Wyman is splitting from Astrid Lindstrum, his girlfriend for fourteen years.

20 September   At a Royal Albert Hall concert in London, fundraising for ARMS, the multiple sclerosis charity, Charlie Watts, Eric Clapton, Steve Winwood, Jeff Beck and Jimmy Page join ex-Face and MS sufferer Ronnie Lane on stage.

30 October   'Undercover Of The Night' is released. A week later the album, *Undercover*, is released on Rolling Stones Records. Three days later the BBC bans the video. The album *reached* No. 1 in the UK.

9 December   Final date of a short US tour to raise cash for ARMS, in New York.

18 December   On his fortieth birthday Keith Richards marries Patti Hansen in Mexico.

1984

23 January   New single 'She Was Hot' is released.

6 May Mick Jagger begins working on a song, 'State Of Shock', with Michael Jackson in New York. It is released in June, reaching No. 3 in the US charts and No. 14 in Britain in July.

29 June *Rewind*, a compilation LP, is released and reaches No. 12 in the UK charts.

August Decca release the *Beggar's Banquet* LP, re-mastered and with its original sleeve.

September Tour plans are postponed because of Mick Jagger's solo schedules. Bill Wyman produces an LP by Willie and the Poor Boys, featuring Charlie Watts and other musicians.

November Band members meet in Amsterdam to discuss their future.

28 November An exhibition of Ronnie Wood's portraits of musicians and friends opens in Dallas. The show runs well into the new year.

1985

4 February Mick Jagger's first solo single, 'Just Another Night', is released in the UK and US. It is taken from his forthcoming album, *She's The Boss* and will reach No. 27 in the UK singles charts.

11 April Just after Mick Jagger begins work on the video for his next single, 'Lucky In Love' (to be released on April 19), the band resume work in Paris on their next album.

13 July The Live Aid concerts take place in London and Philadelphia, broadcast to a global audience of 1.6 billion. The Rolling Stones as such do not take part but Mick, Keith and Ronnie all separately play their parts.

23 August The single of Mick Jagger duetting with David Bowie on 'Dancing In The Street' is released worldwide and becomes a disco classic, thanks partly to an inspired video. It is immediately No. 1 in the UK charts.

18 November Charlie Watts opens for a week at Ronnie Scott's club in London with his 29-piece Big Band. Jack Bruce and Stan Tracey are amongst the musicians.

12 December Ian Stewart, friend, colleague, some-time back-up musician and management stalwart dies of a heart attack in London, aged 47. His funeral on 20 December is attended by all the Rolling Stones. On 23 February 1986 the band played at an invitation-only memorial gig for Ian Stewart at the 100 Club in London.

1986

25 February The Rolling Stones are given a Lifetime Achievement Award at the Grammies in Los Angeles, presented to them by Eric Clapton.

3 March Latest single 'Harlem Shuffle' is released. It will reach No. 7 in the British charts and No. 5 in the USA.

24 March The new album, *Dirty Work*, is released. It enters the British charts in April and will reach No. 3.

19 April The Charlie Watts Orchestra begins a week's engagement at Ronnie Scott's club.

1 May The band convenes at Elstree Studios to shoot a video for their next single, 'One Hit To The Body'. The record is released on 19 May.

20 June Mick Jagger – along with David Bowie, Elton John, Paul McCartney, Phil Collins, Eric Clapton and Tina Turner – takes part in a fundraiser for the Prince's Trust.

5 July Ronnie Wood and Bill Wyman join Rod Stewart on stage for a Faces reunion concert at Wembley.

15/16/17 July Keith Richards joins Bob Dylan for concerts at Madison Square Garden, New York.

31 July Mick Jagger's single 'Ruthless People', theme song for a Disney film of the same name, is released.

29 August A version of 'Jumpin' Jack Flash', recorded by Aretha Franklin and produced by Ronnie and Keith, is released.

15 September Mick discusses plans for his next album with Dave Stewart of the Eurythmics, in Los Angeles. Recording for the album will begin in Holland in November.

November Charlie Watts and his 33-piece orchestra arrive in New York for a short East Coast tour.

1987

21 January Jerry Hall is arrested at the airport in Barbados, charged with importing marijuana.

20 February After two adjournments Jerry Hall is finally found not guilty. She and Mick fly to New York where work on his solo album continues. Both Keith Richards and Ronnie Wood concurrently work on their albums.

13 April Bill Wyman launches his AIMS project in London.

13 June Charlie Watts and his orchestra play at the Playboy Jazz Festival in Hollywood.

13 July Keith discusses a Virgin solo deal with Richard Branson. It is signed on 17 July.

31 August Mick Jagger's single 'Let's Work' is released, reaching No. 35 in UK.

14 September Mick Jagger's album, *Primitive Cool*, is released. It will reach No. 18 in the British charts.

29 October An exhibition of Ronnie Wood's paintings of legendary musicians opens in London. Two days later he flies to Miami, checking progress on his night club and restaurant.

4 November Ronnie Wood opens a North American tour in Columbus, Ohio.

14 November The entire Stones back catalogue is re-released by CBS.

19 December Ronnie Wood and Bo Diddley play at the opening of Woody's On The Beach in Miami.

1988

7/8 January Mick Taylor joins Ronnie onstage at the Miami club.

12 March Mick Jagger and Ronnie Wood meet at the former's hotel in Osaka. Both are in Japan on separate tours. Mick is reputed to receive £1,000,000 for each of his sell-out shows.

25 March By the time the Jagger tour closes in Nagoya, over a quarter of a million tickets have been sold. Before leaving Japan he guests with Tina Turner at her own concert in Osaka.

26 April Mick Jagger is cleared of copyright infringement charges regarding a song called 'Just Another Night', on his *She's The Boss* album.

18 May All five members of the Rolling Stones meet for the first time in two years, at a London hotel. Plans for working together again and touring are discussed.

22 July Bill Wyman's book deal with Viking/Penguin is announced.

26 July Mick Jagger celebrates his 45th birthday and Jerry's first night in *Bus Stop* at a theatre in New Jersey.

22 August Mick Jagger announces the Stones will record and tour together the following year. 'Satisfaction' is voted best single of the last 25 years by *Rolling Stone* magazine.

24 August Upon arrival in Australia for his solo tour Mick Jagger says he will stop touring when he hits fifty.

4 October Virgin release *Talk Is Cheap*, Keith Richards' first solo album.

16 November Ronnie Wood receives undisclosed libel damages after an erroneous newspaper report suggested he had been unfaithful to his wife.

24 November Keith Richards and his band the X-Pensive Winos open their US tour in Atlanta.

1989

January Mick Jagger and Keith Richards plan the new Stones album in Barbados.

18 January At the New York Hall of Fame awards the band is inducted. Bill and Charlie are absent but Mick Taylor joins the others.

19 January Charlie Watts joins Mick, Keith and Ronnie in New York to make plans.

18 February The Stones' financial, legal and business advisers join Jagger and Richards in Barbados. Charlie Watts arrives two days later. Bill is giving a charity concert in Britain but he and Ronnie Wood join the others in early March.

15 March The band sign a multi-million dollar contract – the biggest in rock and roll history – relating to promotion and merchandising of their next tour, for which over fifty dates are proposed.

28 March Recording a new album begins in Montserrat.

31 March Mandy Smith announces her engagement to Bill Wyman.

9 May Party to launch the opening of Bill Wyman's restaurant, Sticky Fingers, in Kensington. Montserrat recordings completed, this month sees the mixing of the new album in London.

17 May A newspaper reports an altercation between Charlie Watts and Mick Jagger, in Amsterdam, where the band have gathered for group discussion.

2 June Bill Wyman marries Mandy Smith quietly in Bury St Edmunds. Three days later the marriage is blessed in London and a reception is held at the Grosvenor House Hotel. Mick Jagger gives the couple a £200,000 Picasso etching.

11 July The Stones announce the Steel Wheels tour at a press conference at Grand Central Station, New York. There will be an album of the same name. Advance ticket sales for the tour break all records. The band and their entourage set up elaborate camp in Washington, Connecticut.

17 August A new single, 'Mixed Emotions', is released. It reaches No. 5 in the US.

31 August Tour opens in Philadelphia. Black market tickets sell for up to forty times the original price.

9 September 'Mixed Emotions' enters the British charts, reaching No. 33.

19 December Final North American date of the tour, in Atlantic City.

1990

February The Stones tour Japan for the first time.

14 February First of the *Steel Wheels* dates in Tokyo.

8 March *Rolling Stone* magazine nominates the Stones as best band and artists of the year for 1989, *Steel Wheels* best album and 'Mixed Emotions' best single. Mick Jagger is nominated best male singer, Bill Wyman best bassist and Charlie Watts best drummer.

22 March Mick Jagger announces the *Urban Jungle* European tour in London. By the following day 120,000 tickets for the Wembley concerts have sold out.

18 May The tour opens in Rotterdam and moves on through France, Germany, Portugal, Spain, Ireland, Italy, Austria, Sweden, Norway and Denmark.

July Release of *Voodoo Lounge* album.

4 July British concerts (between shows in Paris and Dublin), open with several at Wembley and one in Glasgow.

9 August The European leg of the tour closes in Copenhagen.

Sept/Oct The tour continues in Australia.

1991

1 March Julian Temple directs the *Highwire* video in New York.

2 April The Stone's fifth live album, *Flashpoint*, is released.

2 May   The Rolling Stones are honoured at the Ivor Novello Awards in London for their outstanding contribution to British music.

19 November   The Rolling Stones sign to Virgin Records.

10 December   Keith Richards and the X-Pensive Winos' live album is released on CD and video.

1992

20 October   Keith Richards' second solo album, *Main Offender*, is released by Virgin.

27 November   Keith and the Winos begin a short European tour.

31 December   Keith and his band play at a small New York venue.

Bill Wyman and Mandy Smith divorce.

1993

10 January   Ronnie Wood gives the first of four solo concerts in Japan.

17 January   Keith Richards' *Main Offender* tour opens in Seattle.

9 February   Mick Jagger's third solo album, *Wandering Spirit*, is released.

16 February   Bill Wyman stands in for ailing bassist Ronnie Lane at a Faces reunion performance at London's Brit Awards, joining Rod Stewart, Ronnie Wood, Kenney Jones and Ian McLagan onstage.

April   Mick Jagger and Keith Richards fly to Barbados to begin writing songs for a new album and are shortly joined by Charlie Watts.

9 July   The band begin recording in Ireland.

12 October   The Charlie Watts Quintet release their collection *Warm & Tender*.

28 November   Virgin release *Jump Back*, an 18-track greatest hits CD compilation.

1994

January   Bill Wyman leaves the Rolling Stones. Only three original band members remain – but they seem perfectly happy to convene for long tours, even if the days of huge-success in the singles charts are over.

The Rolling Stones pick up an *MTV* Lifetime Achievement Award and a *Billboard* Award for Artistic Excellence.

The two-year *Voodoo Lounge* tour opens.

10 November   The Rolling Stones are the first rock and roll band to broadcast live on the internet.

1995

January   The South American leg of the tour opens with concerts in Mexico and Argentina. Shows in South Africa, Japan and Australasia follow.

3 June   Bob Dylan joins the band onstage in Stockholm for a rendition of 'Like A Rolling Stone'.

30 August   Tour closes in Rotterdam. Live recordings made during the tour form the album *Stripped*, released later in the year.

1996

The Rock 'n' Roll Circus album is released. Charlie Watts' quintet release *Long Ago And Far Away*, an album of jazz and swing classics. Keith Richards works on a solo album.

1997

August   The *Bridges To Babylon* tour is announced.

23 September   Tour opens in Chicago and goes on to thirty-two other cities in North America. Young Leah Wood, Ronnie's daughter, guests with the band when they take the tour to Wembley.

October   Bill Wyman announces the formation of a new band, The Rhythm Kings. Their first album, *Struttin' Our Stuff*, features guest musicians Eric Clapton, Albert Lee, Georgie Fame and Peter Frampton.

16 October   Bill Wyman's first live performance since leaving the Rolling Stones – at the Forum in north London.

8 December   Jerry Hall gives birth to Gabriel Luke Beauregard Jagger in New York – the couple's fourth child and second son.

18 December   It is announced that so far the *Bridges To Babylon* tour of North America has grossed nearly $87 million – a box office record.

1998

23 April   The tour closes with a last show in Chicago – where it had started months earlier.

11 August   The Rolling Stones play in Moscow for the first time.

2 November   The album *No Security*, recorded live at an Amsterdam concert, is released.

1999

January   Jerry Hall files for divorce from Mick Jagger. In the end she won an annulment as the Bali marriage was not recognised by the courts. Afterwards she said Mick's settlement was 'very generous'.

10 June   The Rolling Stones play slightly longer than agreed at a small venue in west London and are fined £50,000 for breaching regulations.

9 July   In a new book, *Death Of A Rolling Stone*, author Anna Wohlin (Brian Jones' girlfriend at the time of his death) asserts that he was murdered.

27 July   DNA tests confirm that Mick Jagger is the father of Luciana Morad's baby son, Lucas.

October   Mick Jagger resumes residence in his former 'marital' home with Jerry Hall. The couple live amicably in separate parts of the house.

13 November   A re-mix of 'It's Only Rock 'n' Roll' is released as a Christmas single, with proceeds going to charity.

26 November   A landlord defeats Mick Jagger and Keith Richards in the High Court after the Stones attempt to sue him for exploitation because he named his pub 'Rolling Stone'.

2000

3 January '(I Can't Get No) Satisfaction' topped a US poll of the 100 greatest rock songs of all time.

16 January A spokesman for Britain's Prime Minister Tony Blair denies that Downing Street had vetoed a knighthood for Mick Jagger in the Queen's New Year's honours, in which both Elton John and Paul McCartney were knighted.

28 March Mick Jagger returns to his old school Dartford Grammar to open a new arts centre named after him.

May Mick, Ronnie, Charlie and Keith play at a private pub gig in south London – a wake for the band's long-term employee Joe Seabrook who had died shortly before, aged 58.

27 May Band members convene at the funeral of Eva Jagger, Mick's 87 year-old mother.

3 July Mick Jagger and Marsha Hunt attend the wedding of their daughter Karis, in San Francisco.

2 December Jade Jagger and her two children survive a car crash near their home in Ibiza. Both Mick and Bianca Jagger rush to them and charter a jet to take them to Britain for treatment.

Jerry Hall appears as Mrs Robinson in *The Graduate* in London's West End.

2001

August Bono, Pete Townsend and Missy Elliott, amongst others, join Mick Jagger in the studio as he records his next solo album, *Goddess In The Doorway*.

23 October Mick Jagger announces that the Stones will tour again – but first he has to promote *Goddess In The Doorway*.

2002

May A new Rolling Stones tour is announced in New York. It is set to open in Boston in September.

31 May Plans for The Rolling Stones Remastered series are announced. Twenty-two classic albums, various compilations and some singles are to be re-formatted for today's advanced home music technology.

9 June Michael Phillip Jagger is knighted for services to music in the Queen's Golden Jubilee Birthday honours.

1 October The band releases their greatest hits album, *Forty Licks* which contains four new songs.

2003

November The band plays their first concert in Hong Kong as part of Harbour Fest- an effort to revive the Hong Kong economy after the effects of SARS.

2005

21 August The Rolling Stones begin their Bigger Bang world tour.

5 September *A Bigger Bang* is released. It is the Rolling Stone's 22nd studio album.

2006

26 April Keith Richards receives a minor head injury when he falls out of a tree in Fiji.

November The Bigger Bang tour is named the highest grossing tour ever, netting $437 million.

2007

10 June The band make their first festival appearance in 30 years at the Isle of Wight Festival.

2 October Mick Jagger releases his solo work, 'The Very Best of Mick Jagger.'

2008

17 January The Rolling Stones announce they are leaving EMI/ Virgin Records to sign with Universal Music Group/ UMG.

4 April Shine a Light is released. The film, directed by Martin Scorsese, documented two performances that the band did at New York's Beacon Theatre in 2006.

April Shine a Light soundtrack is released.

2010

23 May *Exile on Main St* is reissued, going straight to No. 1 in the UK charts, almost 38 years to the week after it first occupied that position. In the US the album re-entered the charts at No. 2.

11 October *Ladies and Gentlemen: The Rolling Stones* is released in cinemas and later on DVD.

26 Oct Keith's autobiography, *Life*, is released.

Acknowledgments

The photographs for this book are from the archives of the *Daily Mail*.

Particular thanks to Steve Torrington and Alan Pinnock,
without whose help this book would not have been possible.